Accountancy

Sarah Perrin is a freelance journalist specialising in business and finance. She writes for a wide range of professional and business magazines and acted as occasional editor of the City diary of London's *Evening Standard*. After completing a degree in Philosophy, Politics and Economics, she qualified as a chartered accountant with Arthur Andersen in London, before spending a year travelling and temping. She moved into journalism during three years as a reporter for leading trade weekly *Accountancy Age*.

Accountancy

Sarah Perrin

FOURTH ESTATE • *London*

First published in Great Britain in 1999 by
Fourth Estate Limited
6 Salem Road
London W2 4BU

Copyright © 1999 Fourth Estate Limited

10 9 8 7 6 5 4 3 2 1

The right of Sarah Perrin to be identified as the author of this work has been asserted by her in accordance with the Copyright, Designs and Patents Act 1988.

ISBN 1-85702-751-5

All rights reserved. No part of this publication may be reproduced, transmitted, or stored in a retrieval system, in any form or by any means, without permission in writing from Fourth Estate Limited.

Typeset by York House Typographic Ltd, London
Printed in Great Britain by Clays Ltd, St Ives plc, Bungay, Suffolk

Contents

Introduction   **1**

1   First Impressions   **8**

The modern accountant's working life – Life in practice – Industry – Banking and the City – The public sector – Working routines

2   Breaking in   **36**

Personal qualities – Levels of entry – Simplifying the decision process – The qualification maze – Accountancy bodies – Specialist qualifications – Your first employer – Industry – Public sector – The applications process

3   Onwards and Upwards   **69**

The upward path – Mobility – Specialisation – Career planning and job hunting – Getting creative – Equal opportunities – The rewards – The frustrations

4   Snakes and Ladders   **93**

The changing environment – Staying fresh – Temporary career options – Interim management – Transferability of skills

5   Opportunities Abroad   **105**

Accountants in practice – Industry and commerce –

Public sector – Voluntary Service Overseas – Finding that overseas position – Career impact – And finally . . .

Appendix A: **Qualifications**	**116**
Appendix B: **Accountancy Degrees**	**133**
Appendix C: **Useful Addresses**	**141**
Appendix D: **Further Reading**	**145**

Introduction

'Accountants are the witch-doctors of the modern world and willing to turn their hands to any kind of magic.'
Lord Justice Harman, February 1964

It takes a lively mind to fit witch-doctors and accountants into the same box. Witch-doctors inspire fear and respect in their community. They are seen as having the power of life and death. Their potions and spells are secret from the ordinary man or woman. Can the same be said of accountants?

In some ways, yes. Accountants have traditionally been respected for their financial expertise, and they may inspire fear when on the hunt for fraudsters. It is only in recent times that, along with other professionals, their reputation has been tarnished by the mud that flies from high-profile scandals. Accountants may also wield the power of life and death over companies, if not individuals, since some specialist accountants can decide when a company has to be wound up. Finally, many of the accountant's spells, the jargon and theory, are mystifying to the financially naïve. 'Deferred tax', 'Accruals', 'Share Premium Account'. What does this all mean?

There the similarities end. Witch-doctors are a rare breed. Accountants thrive everywhere. The largest UK accountancy body, the Institute of Chartered Accountants in England & Wales, has over 111,000 members world-wide, though the vast majority of those work in the UK. Considering all the members of other bodies, accountants probably make up around 1 per cent of the UK work-force.

Many accountants are to be found working in practice. This

doesn't mean they are still getting their skills up to speed. It means they work in professional audit and accounting partnerships and the largest of these are comparable to multinational companies. Total fee income from the UK accountancy sector is expected to be around £7.39 billion in 1997, and it's rising. By the year 2001, the accountancy market could be worth almost £9.5 billion.

Other accountants work within companies, controlling their finances and helping to shape corporate strategies. Charities need them too, as do hospitals, local government and even churches. They staff the gleaming skyscrapers of London's City banks. They do the sums that raise the funding for the British movie industry. Pick almost any organisation, then spot the accountant.

The range of environments in which accountants can work gives the profession a huge variety. If you are attracted by billion-pound figures, fast-moving deals and City culture, then follow the road to becoming a corporate financier helping to facilitate the purchase or sale of major companies. If you are interested in the arts, then you could work for the Arts Council, Royal Opera House, or Manchester's Bridgewater Hall, managing the finances and juggling the need for creative spending with the need to balance the books.

The range of roles that accountants fulfil during their working days is also staggering. The accountancy profession starts with the need to prepare financial accounts that show how organisations have spent their income, whether they have made a profit or a loss. Companies, charities, banks and other institutions are bound by law to report their financial performance publicly. The precise requirements for what is reported vary, but the accounts show outsiders a picture of how the organisation has performed. Those outsiders might be shareholders, banks who have lent a business money, or government bodies.

Once the accounts have been prepared, other accountants are then needed to check that the reported figures are accurate. External auditors, accountants who work in public practice, are brought in to decide whether a client's accounts show a 'true and fair' view. Other in-house staff, known as internal auditors, may also be used to check that the company's accounting and other systems are working properly, to minimise the chance that the company will get its figures wrong. Internal auditors also try to prevent fraud, installing control systems that make it harder for employees or directors to steal from the business undetected.

Management accountants have yet another role. They are needed to produce data that is useful for taking management decisions about the future direction of a business or organisation. For example, imagine that the Tesco supermarket chain wants to expand a store. What products should it choose to stock the new space? Management accountants could be used to analyse profit margins on different stock lines, perhaps using data from other stores and building in variations for regional preferences. What if a company wants to review its asset replacement policy, perhaps using its factory machinery for an extra six months before renewal? Management accountants could forecast the potential impact of such a change, considering factors such as repair costs during the life of the asset: how rapidly do repair costs increase towards the end of the asset's life? Would the company lose out on scrap value? Would it be able to reduce immediate borrowings at the bank?

Sometimes an organisation's management may need specialist advice that its in-house accounting team cannot provide, perhaps on tax or fund-raising issues. It may seek this advice from the accountancy firm that audits its books. Individuals pay tax as well as companies and may also need advice on how to complete tax forms and comply with legal requirements while minimising the tax bill. It is to an accountant they will look for that advice.

If a business really gets into trouble it may have to call in corporate recovery experts, also known as insolvency practitioners. They will assess the viability of the business, its chances of recovering to trade successfully in future. They may be appointed as administrators, to steer the business through to profitability again, perhaps restructuring its operations and debts. They may have to sell the business off as a going concern, or liquidate it – close it down and sell off individual assets to raise cash to pay off the company's debts.

Corporate finance has to be one of the most demanding and dramatic areas that accountants move into. To thrive requires considerable experience. The role demands a sharp business head and a nose for a good deal. You may be acting for clients looking to buy up a company in a drive for expansion. You have to be able to spot target companies to buy, approach them about doing a deal, estimate a reasonable price, negotiate for the best outcome for your clients, then make sure that the target company's projected figures represent its performance accurately. This side of the work, the due diligence, is similar to the audit role in that it requires gaining reasonable assurance that no nasty holes will appear in the company's finances after purchase. Some corporate financiers advise companies on how to raise funds for expansion. Others invite investors to pay cash into specific funds designed to invest in high growth companies. They then have to find the right companies for the investment. Other banking and City jobs require young accountants to monitor the performance of traders, checking controls are working properly, and ensuring the organisation doesn't breach any regulations.

Moving further from the straight accountancy role takes you to management consultancy. The giant audit firms have expanded far from their origins, offering advice on the full range of business issues – human resource management, information systems, marketing, supply-chain management, the works. Accountants can move across into these broader areas if they have the flair and gain the relevant business-oriented experience.

You do not need to be sure when you start out on your accountancy career exactly where you want to end up, but your starting-point may affect your decisions along the way. Sometimes an individual's plans change with greater experience. Accountancy is such a broad professional church that twists and turns are quite possible to achieve. For example, certainly during their training period, and even after, auditors spend much of their time working at clients' offices rather than the office of their own firm. There may be considerable travel

Introduction

involved, to clients' subsidiaries, factories or warehouses. At the end of a three-year training contract some newly qualified auditors have had enough of all that racing around and decide to move into their firm's tax division. Though they will still need to develop an understanding of their clients' affairs, there will be far less need to visit far-flung client sites. Head office should be the main source of client data and most of the tax calculation and consulting work will be performed at the accountancy practice's own office.

If accountancy is a flexible career, then so must accountants themselves be flexible. In the old days, an accountant's life could have been described as generally slow moving. Historical transactions were recorded with pen and ink in thick ledgers. It was a safe and secure profession, well paid and well respected. Today's accountant will be working in a fast-paced environment. If companies are changing hands, it may be necessary to work through the night to get the deal done. There is no time for slackness if derivatives, complex financial products, are being traded in the City and the back-room accountant has to reconcile the day's figures. If he misses something, and controls are breached, billions of pounds of a client's or investors' money could be lost.

To keep up with fast-moving transactions and to manipulate all the data needed for management decisions, computers are now an everyday essential. If you enter the profession today, it won't be long before a spreadsheet is sitting on your PC screen. And because the accountancy profession essentially serves the business community, the arts world, the NHS and government bodies, it has to deal with the changing requirements of those organisations. That can mean increasing opportunities. For example, the introduction of internal markets into the NHS required accountants for their implementation. Tighter controls on public spending and emphasis on efficient financial management in the NHS and other areas of the public sector had the same effect. But a change of political emphasis could just as well shut down those opportunities again. Even in the private sector, jobs for life are a rare thing. Far more accountants now move regularly between accountancy firms or between companies, looking for promotion, new challenges, or better pay. Accountancy is as tough a world as any for those who allow their skills to become outdated, or who let their professional standards slip. Those who do keep up to scratch, who become expert in areas of current demand, who are familiar with IT and are good communicators, can look forward to excellent financial rewards and high levels of job satisfaction.

Professor Sir David Tweedie is the chairman of the Accounting Standards Board, the body empowered to set the accounting rules for the UK. That position makes him one of the most influential accountants in the UK profession and he also represents the UK on the international accounting stage. He didn't intend to become an accountant, but qualified with the Institute of Chartered Accountants of Scotland in 1972.

Tweedie's career has mixed academia with life in the profession. After completing a Ph.D. in Management and Incomes Policy at the University of Edinburgh in 1969, he trained as a chartered accountant with a firm in Glasgow. Returning to Edinburgh University in 1972, he lectured for five years before moving to the Institute of Chartered Accountants of Scotland as Technical Director. In 1982 he joined one of the large accountancy firms, KMG Thomson McLintock (a previous incarnation of Big Six firm KPMG), as National Research Partner, later becoming National Technical Partner. He took up his post at the ASB in 1990. Despite his unwilling start, he now highly recommends the benefits that come with an accountancy training and qualification:

I didn't want to be a CA [chartered accountant]. My old man took me off to meet one – I shot off and went and did a Ph.D. instead. But in the end I enjoyed it, though not in the first year. The chartered accountancy training is excellent and when you start to have control of jobs you start getting a lot of enjoyment out of it. I found four to five frauds during my apprenticeship. The best thing I did was to train in chartered accountancy. After that I was given opportunities because of the other things I had done – the Ph.D. made me slightly different. But having the CA after your name pays the bills.

The beauty of accountancy is that being financially literate is very useful. I know lots and lots of managers who are terrified of accountants – accountants can't be fooled. I think everyone should have some financial training. The country would be a better place. Accountancy is also internationally transportable. You can travel with 60 per cent of your basic knowledge intact. Broadly speaking, we all talk the same financial language. That means you can work anywhere you like. Accountancy opens lots and lots of doors.

1 First Impressions

It's probably fair to say that accountants have a bit of an image problem. Think Monty Python, think John Cleese. The street credibility of accountants across the land suffered a lingering blow the day the Python team broadcast a sketch about one particular accountant who went to see a careers guidance counsellor. The accountant wanted a change of scene, excitement, a job that would let him live! He wanted to become a lion tamer. Needless to say, he was persuaded to think about moving into banking instead, though he didn't have enough nerve to be able to make the actual decision to do so. Accountancy, the viewers were told, was a debilitating social disease. The message was clear. The life of an accountant is dull. Accountants are dull people.

If you choose a career in accountancy, there is a fair bet you will meet people who will look at you with an incredulous expression and ask you why you did it. In the early years, when you are training, studying for exams and doing the less skilled work, you may ask yourself the same question. Be ready for this and accept it. Don't forget that the early years in many jobs have their dull moments. In some fields these dull moments don't decrease. But in accountancy, everyone agrees that the higher you get, the more interesting the work becomes. There are hundreds of thousands of accountants who have studied, trained and now enjoy a fulfilling career. They can't all be wrong. But what exactly do they do?

THE MODERN ACCOUNTANT'S WORKING LIFE

Accountancy began with the need to record and explain financial transactions. Accounting is essentially a language designed to do just that. It centres around numbers, rather than words, but it is still a method of communication. Accountants are the communicators and the interpreters of that language. Wherever they work, that language forms a common thread.

Accountancy is very much a white-collar career and accountants are primarily office workers. That doesn't mean they spend their whole time stuck behind a desk. External auditors have to get out and about, meeting clients. Internal auditors may have to travel around their company's offices, within the UK and abroad.

Since almost every type of organisation needs accountants, it is impossible to define their natural habitat. It could be the City skyscraper with tinted glass windows, or it could be the spare room at the back of the house of the self-employed independent accountant. The largest accountancy firms and the major corporations may have glossy offices, perhaps with internal gyms, bars and restaurants. Smaller organisations will have fewer frills but possibly a cosier working atmosphere. There is enough scope for all types of personality to find the working conditions that suit them.

One pretty inescapable fact, however, is that the accountant's dress code lies at the conservative end of the business couture range. Advertising executives may display a little more individuality in their style of clothing, but for most accountants, traditional business attire is the rule. For men, suits and ties, generally dark and frequently pinstriped. For women, suits are also the norm. Trousers may or may not be acceptable, depending on the organisation. Some auditing firms believe their clients prefer female auditors to wear skirts. A small minority of organisations may have a relaxed attitude to dress, allowing more casual wear, but it's generally true that even in the arty worlds of publishing or design, while the journalists and designers may wear jeans or even shorts, the finance team will be in jacket and tie.

Though the historical image of accountancy may involve rows of individuals seated at high desks writing lists of figures with quill pens, today's financial world is increasingly high tech. Computers have revolutionised the accounting world just as they have most other working environments. It would be virtually impossible to avoid using computers in an accounting role. Almost every company and individual in business now maintains computerised accounts using spreadsheets and databases to record and control financial transactions. The payroll clerk, the finance director and the auditor all use computer programmes developed to make their own jobs more efficient.

Audit firms and companies will have some systems designed specifically for their own purposes. For example, audit firms now make wide use of IT packages to help them identify risk areas when auditing clients. Auditors and management accountants use spreadsheets to manipulate data. For example, costs associated with an operating unit could be shown on a spreadsheet and sorted to show all items above a minimum amount. Those items could be investigated to see if they are justified, or whether they can be reduced in future. Spreadsheets also make budgeting far simpler, allowing the accountant to see the impact of different costs or revenues on projected year-end figures. There are a huge range of packages on the market, but common ones include Excel for spreadsheets and Sage, SAP and Oracle for financial packages. For communicating with colleagues and clients, packages such as Microsoft Word and Lotus Notes are standard. Employers will train you in the skills relevant to your level and role, keeping you updated as systems change. You do not need to have a deep interest in computers, but you do need to be comfortable working with them. Technophobes should look elsewhere or master their fear of IT quickly. You won't get far without it.

One assumption most people would probably make is that accountancy and glamour don't go together. This is not entirely true. Even within accountancy there is the potential to satisfy those partial to a bit of glitz. What do pop stars and famous actresses do with their money? They probably won't know how best to invest it and will need an accountant to help them. Unfortunately for Sting, his accountant Keith Moore didn't behave with the honesty required of the profession and was convicted of stealing over £6 million from the tantric pop star. But glamour comes in many forms. It may be found simply in the buzz of working in the City, close to the centre of Europe's biggest financial market. But to be fair, most accountants probably aren't looking for glamour in their work. The management accountant at a steel-pipe factory on an industrial estate in Stoke-on-Trent probably didn't have glamour on his list of priorities when choosing his job.

What is undeniably true is that anarchists won't feel at home working in accountancy. The promotional ladder in many organisations remains fairly rigid and those at the top expect respect. How rigid that hierarchy is will vary from one employer to another, determined partly by the size of the firm. The largest accountancy firms, which have hundreds of partners, thousands of staff and UK fee income well over the half-billion-pound mark, have a fairly traditional structure, with partners at the top and trainees at the bottom. The two groups may interact relatively little. Offices are large and partners' time costs money. Smaller organisations, with two or three partners and fees of several hundred thousand pounds, may have a more relaxed atmosphere and structure, though again accountancy firms will still have trainees at one end of the power scale and partners at the other and many steps in between. In accountancy firms big and small, managers and partners will have their own offices. More junior levels usually share open-plan space, often with no specified desk allocated to them. The open-plan layout is common in industry too, though again managerial grades will have their own offices.

Accountants are generally a highly sociable group of people. That sociability is helped by the exam-based training that lies at the start of many accounting careers. The way the large accounting firms recruit trainee staff creates an atmosphere rather like that at school or college in the sense that people feel they belong to a particular intake. Trainees starting their contracts on the same day attend induction courses together. Those in the same year often go to the same exam courses.

Perhaps because the need to pass exams puts people under considerable and shared stress, members of the same intake often stay in touch for years after, even when they have left their training firm long behind. In small firms, that peer-group support may be less noticeable, particularly if you are the only trainee taken on that year.

It is worth noting that because so many young accountants start their training straight after university, late entrants to the profession may feel slightly out of place. It is also probably fair to say that the further you get from your mid-twenties, the harder it will be to become a trainee auditor. There are several reasons for this. Although the accountancy firms have no stated policies to rule out older applicants, they see more of a gamble in taking on late starters. As one recruiting partner explained, some more mature trainees prove to be great successes. Because they are older, they have no desire to waste time by failing their exams, so they study harder. They also bring with them greater breadth of experience which may equip them well for dealing with clients. But on the downside, those who haven't taken any exams for some years may find the whole experience far harder than they expect. They may also have to face a pay cut, depending on their previous employment.

In the corporate world, the degree of peer-group binding again depends on the size of the company. A small finance department will offer fewer colleagues to share a pint on a Friday evening. Departments with older staff may be less willing to socialise after hours at all. But these are factors that apply to many management functions, not just accounting and finance.

One major dampener on the trainee accountant's social life is the studying that has to be done for exams. Only the brightest sparks will get through their professional exams without disciplined study. Some trainees will have to study in the evenings while doing their normal day job. Others will be sent off on block-release courses, but there will still be homework and revision to do at night. Passing the exams takes dedication and the ability to reject invitations from your non-accountant friends heading to the pub. If you are the kind of social animal who just can't refuse such temptations, say no to accounting.

Higher up the accountancy ladder, the amount of work-based socialising varies hugely. Accountants in practice may be expected to put on social events for clients, which might entail booking a box for a one-day international at Lord's or a simple lunch.

Perhaps because many people expect accountancy to be a rather stolid, unsurprising existence, surveys have found it to be one of the most stressful occupations in the financial services sector. Stress levels have also increased over the last twelve years. Stress is no respecter of seniority and can crop up at all levels. Research shows that lack of control is one of the key contributing factors; this can apply just as readily to the head of the finance department (who, though controlling the department, will have to report to other bosses, such as the chief executive or the shareholders) as to the most exam-pressurised trainee.

Accountants may simply be stressed because they work hard. According to a survey by recruiters Robert Half International, the average working week in accountancy is 47.2 hours, with 40 per cent of staff working over fifty hours a week. Even worse, 60 per cent take work home in the evenings and at weekends. Most accountants don't have a particularly easy life, so if that's what you want, look elsewhere. Nor is accountancy the type of career where you are likely to get a job and just sit there until retirement. Around half of newly qualifieds think about changing their employer soon after qualification. The encouraging news is that only three out of ten say they would like to change careers.

Accountants find encouragement to persevere with accountancy from the typical pay and benefits they enjoy. Graduates who gain one of the respected accountancy qualifications three years into their careers can earn salaries from £20,000 to £30,000 plus, depending on location and the type of work. West Country auditors will lie in the lower end of the range, while accountants in the merchant banks of the City of London will be at the upper end. A few years on, the rewards can be excellent. Finance directors in growing companies and partners in medium-sized firms can top the £100,000 mark, while those in senior positions in the largest organisations can double or triple that. Finally, there are the added perks of pension contributions, company cars and share options to keep almost all qualified accountants smiling.

LIFE IN PRACTICE

The accountancy practices have been one of the main training sources for the UK's accountants. Even those who later move into industry or banking, charities or the public sector, may well have started their accounting life in an audit firm. In the 1990s there is movement back the other way too, as the firms seek to develop specialist expertise in particular industrial sectors. Accountants who qualified in industry may find themselves highly valued by an audit and consulting firm.

Accountancy firms, with the exception of KPMG Audit plc, are not companies. They are partnerships. Traditionally this meant that partners, who had bought a stake in the firm, were remunerated by receiving a share of the year's profits. These days there tend to be two types of partners. Equity partners, those who own a stake in the firm, each month draw an agreed sum based on expected profits. The balance of their share of the final profit is paid out at the end of the year. Salaried partners start out as they are termed – on a salary, much like an ordinary employee. However, after perhaps a year, that salary will be calculated on a profit-share basis, and a final bonus may be added on top.

Partners form the highest level of management in the firm. In large firms they will be specialists in either audit, tax, insolvency, corporate finance or consulting. In smaller general practices they will tend to have a broader base to their work, covering both audit and tax issues.

The audit is the bread-and-butter work of the firms. Every UK limited company above a certain size must appoint an auditor to report on its accounts. The largest audits involve huge teams of staff of different grades. At the top is the partner who has the ultimate responsibility for signing off, or approving, a set of a client's accounts. Below the partner is the manager who has a closer involvement in the organisation of the audit, though often in a highly supervisory role. He will have to report back to the partner if anything goes wrong. He will review the audit files prepared by more junior staff.

The person with the key hands-on role in the daily running of the audit assignment is generally called a 'senior'. The senior will be part or fully qualified with two or more years' audit experience. At the bottom of the pile are the junior staff, often called assistants, usually in their first two years with the firm.

The senior will often do most of the planning before the audit starts, estimating how many staff will be needed, using the experience of previous audits and taking into account any changes affecting the client during the year. If, for example, the client has bought another company, that will certainly mean more work. If it has changed its computer systems, they will need to be considered for reliability. Much of the planning involves assessing the degree of risk attached to different parts of the company's financial statements. Has it a bad record of collecting its debts? Did the finance director leave at short notice under a cloud? The impact of computer systems will be considered – is it possible to download data from the client's computer systems? How reliable are the client's computer systems anyway?

Once the audit is under way, the senior has to direct the junior staff on the job. That could mean explaining basic audit procedures to the most junior members of the team. The audit work will have to be adjusted to take account of unexpected findings. For example, poor controls for recording cash receipts could mean introducing more extensive tests on cash balances. All audit work is documented in detailed audit files. Seniors review the work of the junior staff. Managers review the files again, including the work of the senior, before passing the files on to the partner.

During the audit, the team may need to co-ordinate with other departments of its firm, such as the tax team who may want to check data needed for tax calculations. The tax department will be organised along similar lines to the audit group, though staff spend far more time in their own office.

In contrast to auditors, the work of other departments within the firm is not so structured around a regular annual event. One area where the unexpected is the norm is corporate recovery, or insolvency. Staff may arrive at the office in the morning and be sent straight out to shut down a company that has become insolvent. The excitement is high but the work can be personally demanding. It takes a particularly strong personality to turn up at a factory and tell the staff to go home, that the company may be shut down and that they may have no jobs to come back to.

If there is some doubt over the viability of a company, it may go into administrative receivership. The insolvency team may go in and effectively take over the running of the business themselves. The existing management may be needed for advice, but the decisions are taken by the insolvency team. The job requires people who can learn fast about how different industries work and who can persuade suspicious, anxious staff at client companies to work with them.

Sometimes the insolvency team will be on notice that they may be about to be called in. When the activities of Nick Leeson, the trader whose massive losses brought down Barings Bank, were uncovered, Ernst & Young put huge numbers of staff on standby. Over the course of a weekend it became clear that Barings was in serious trouble and late on the Sunday night the Bank of England appointed E&Y to take over. Staff mobilised, flooding into Barings to check over the accounts and keep the bank operational until a sale was negotiated.

Corporate finance is another area of brisk, often very competitive, deal-making. Even with these high-drama events, the accountant still has to do a lot of detailed work. Documentation is vital. There is no allowance for sloppiness. Accountants can be sued for damages if it can be proved they have not acted in accordance with best practice as established by their regulatory bodies, and that their negligence has caused a client to suffer a loss. If, for example, company A buys company B and then finds that there was a massive error in company B's accounts, company A will want to know why. Company A will look at every possible way to recover some of its lost money. If the accountancy firm that advised on the purchase can't show that it did everything by the book and carried out every check expected of it to verify the figures and documented all those activities thoroughly, a court battle and a big bill could be heading its way.

Forensic accounting is a rapidly growing area in the largest audit firms, and in specialist firms who do no other work. Forensic accounting is the equivalent of the forensic detective work so favoured in the novels of Patricia Cornwell and other crime writers – it involves picking over any and all relevant company data in an attempt either to prove errors in the work conducted by another firm, or to prove the validity of the work done, or uncover a fraud, or to pin a fraud on an individual or group of individuals. The work may lead to the accountant appearing as a prosecution witness in court. This expert-witness dimension to the job requires people with cool, calm personalities who can explain potentially complex accounting issues to a lay jury.

CASE STUDY

Danielle Stewart, aged thirty-five, is a partner in the small London accountancy firm of Warrener Stewart and specialises in owner-managed businesses (OMBs). She has become a renowned expert in the field and plays a major role in shaping the future of small-business auditing and accounting through her involvement in numerous professional committees. One of her major achievements was to design and market the first computerised small company audit system, now in use in over 500 firms of auditors and sixteen countries. In 1994 she was voted Young Accountant of the Year. After her A levels she completed an Accountancy Foundation Course at Kingston University.

I went into accountancy because I wanted to do something where I could be sure of earning a living, whatever happened. People will always need accountants. Even if we had a nuclear holocaust and people were trading food, there would have to be a system for adding it up.

I started training with a small firm which I joined because there were family connections. But I left after my first professional exams because

Accountancy

I wanted to gain experience of larger audits. I joined Halpen & Woolf which had some great plc audits. It was good experience – I got exposure to some very good audit methodologies and experience of accounts preparation.

Not long after qualification, I decided I wanted some different experience and got excited about an entertainment-based firm in Covent Garden. But I stayed there only six months because the work was very tax-based with almost no auditing. I had some very exciting names as clients, but the work didn't suit me. So I joined Bright Grahame Murray, a firm in the top forty in the country. They had a good smattering of listed audit clients. I rose to be senior audit manager and I really enjoyed my work. I was running quite big teams of people there. I probably would have stayed and become a partner but Peter Warrener came along and tempted me away. Peter had set up his own accounting firm five years before, concentrating on contract work, acquisitions and mergers. He brought me in to build up the audit side and we set up as Warrener Stewart. We now employ seven accountants, and have two other partners and a turnover of approximately £700,000.

There have been moments when I regretted the move. The hardest part was going from an environment where I had my own team of seven staff and others I could borrow, to a situation where I was doing everything myself. But I viewed it as a positive thing that I could set up the first audit files for clients properly. Another hard aspect was feeling so unsupported. Peter was not an expert in my field. I was very young to be in that situation. There was a lot of stress. I would throw files at the walls and scream. My first marriage broke up. I was working until nine at night and one day every weekend. Setting up on your own is worth it in the long run but it takes it out of you. I have more balance in my life now. I leave the office at 6.30 p.m. and I enjoy spending time with my young daughter.

The thing I liked the most about the change was not being answerable to anybody. I didn't have to justify anything to anyone. The biggest advantage now is the freedom it gives me to pursue my academic and regulatory interests in the profession. I am now an acknowledged expert on the audit of OMBs. I am famous in the profession, and I enjoy that. On balance, I guess I couldn't have a nicer life.

My ambition now is to continue to develop Warrener Stewart as the pre-eminent firm of accountants in the OMB sector, in terms of how we are regarded and our standards. Later on I wouldn't mind a stint as

President of the ICAEW. I see myself retiring by the age of fifty-five and maybe writing books and changing the world.

Accountancy is a good career for women, better than any I know. There is virtually no prejudice in the practice side, though there may be some in industry. I did find prejudice about being young when I tried to tell people what they should do, but almost none through being a woman.

To be successful, in terms of being a good business adviser, you need to have high standards so that you are not prepared to compromise. There are always people who will pay for quality. Secondly, you have to be prepared to work very hard at times. And third, you have to be a good communicator.

My advice to people considering accountancy is never to think of it as a soft option. It has been harder than I ever imagined, every step of the way, from sitting the exams through to setting up in practice. If you want an easy life, don't become an accountant.

CASE STUDY

Mavis Sargent, aged sixty-five, left school at sixteen and joined the Inland Revenue, working in her local tax office. She has worked in tax throughout her career, gaining her tax qualifications along the way and then studying with the ACCA as a mature entrant. She now chairs the ACCA's taxation committee.

I backed into accountancy. I was born in 1932 and lived in Doncaster in South Yorkshire, surrounded by mining villages, where the career expectations for women were not high. The men went into the mines and the women did what they could find. When I left school, the Inland Revenue was recruiting locally and since I was good at maths, I applied. I stayed with the Revenue for six years, but left when I married.

It was at that point, in 1954, that I first entered the profession, setting up a tax department for a local firm of chartered accountants in Doncaster. After my first baby, I did the same thing for a certified practice. In this period of my life, I moved around the country with my family and so worked for a variety of small and medium-sized practices, doing a mix of work, but concentrating largely on tax. Before training with the ACCA, I did my ATII and then the FTII, the exams set by the

Chartered Institute of Tax. Then I enrolled with the ACCA in 1971, qualifying in 1973. Whilst I had acquired a lot of understanding about accounts, I recognised the benefits of having a formal qualification. I felt you couldn't really do tax properly without a thorough knowledge of accounts. I now chair the ACCA's tax committee. I got involved with the Association very soon after I qualified.

In around 1976 I joined the Confederation of British Industry and ran its tax department for a couple of years. It was a policy rather than a technical post and it was great fun, but I thought if you stayed in that line too long you would lose an awful lot of technical knowledge. So I went back into practice. I now have a continuing, flexible working arrangement with the firm of Moore Stephens, where I was a London tax partner for just over three years, but now I pretty much do my own thing. I have a mix of international clients, and advise other practices.

I tried very hard throughout my working life to stay involved with every side of tax and not get too specialised. It's a very difficult thing to do, particularly within a large practice. At Moore Stephens I was a consultancy partner, which meant I didn't have compliance work but rather I handled one-off problems for clients. I do think it's necessary to have some people who cover the whole tax spectrum. It's rare that you get a problem that is wholly about corporate tax, or wholly personal. You could solve someone's inheritance-tax worries, but cause a problem somewhere else.

I have lived all over the country and what I would say about tax is, it is always there. You can always turn your hand to it. Even when things were tight in the profession, there were always jobs for tax people. It's a job you have to like, but if you do, it's immensely flexible. It also tends to be better paid than other areas of accountancy. I never felt I had any problems at all as a woman. I think it's like any other profession – if you are reasonably good at it, it doesn't matter. There have been many occasions when, if I looked around a room, I was the only woman there, but I think there are plenty of opportunities.

INDUSTRY

If you have a preference for being close to the action, you may prefer to train in an industrial environment. The finance department of a plc, typically led and staffed by accountants, plays a key role in determining the company's success. The team, led by the finance director, is responsible for both inputting the financial element to strategic decisions, and for presenting the company's results. That strategic element, which many finance professionals find the most rewarding part of the job, is on the increase. The scale of the strategy in question may vary from the minor tinkering in production processes to questions of corporate take-overs.

For example, the finance team might evaluate the viability of investing in new plant and machinery – should new assets be purchased now or in two years' time? What is the optimum period of time that a production line can keep running before faults become too frequent and therefore costly? If the company is seeking to expand its sales network, the finance team may have to predict the impact of sudden extra salary costs on cash flow. At what rate can staff safely be taken on? One particular product has been generating low returns. Should the company change its product mix to increase production of a similar line which brings in a higher margin? The biggest decisions could concern whether to acquire another business, or sell a subsidiary. The finance team will have to assess the impact on the value of the business. Will shareholder value be increased or not?

All these decisions, whether forecasting the impact of an action or budgeting for future production, require close liaison with other departments. Different departments will not always see things the same way. The sales department, chasing a bonus, may want to increase sales at all costs. The finance department may argue that a product is losing money, and production should be slowed. Whatever the issue, the finance team has a key role to play in making sure that the company's strategy is financially sound.

Not everyone in the team will be involved in this form of work. Administrative and compliance issues, making sure that VAT returns are made on time and accounts filed, takes up the time of many finance staff. However, the potential is there to get involved in more commercial work for those with the ambition.

Reporting the company's performance is another key responsibility of the finance director. The company's financial results make a statement about the company's performance and hint at its potential future development. City analysts will use information in the accounts to make judgements about the company – whether it should be recommended to investors, how well it is likely to do. If a company gets the thumbs down, the share price can fall, and along with it the company's value.

You might think that it isn't the finance department's fault if the results are bad. To a certain extent, that is true. There may be little the finance director can do if a product becomes outdated or the weather turns so foul that no one buys ice-cream for a whole summer. But one of the challenges facing the finance director is to make the best use of any options available in order to present glowing results. Accounting isn't a science. When preparing accounts, companies have to follow broad principles and guidance set by the accounting authorities, but within those guidelines there is scope to 'massage' the results, depending on exactly what accounting policies they use. There have been many cases of companies influencing their profits by many millions simply by changing the way they account for the cost of using assets in the business. For example, a company may have been charging the cost of its assets against profits over a period of ten years, creating an expense of, say, £100,000 a year. By changing its policy so that assets are charged over a period of fifteen years, the annual expense could immediately be cut by two thirds, boosting profits. This is a simple accounting manipulation. Many are more complex but the whole lot, lumped under the term 'creative accounting', have brought the profession into disrepute. Dodgy accounting practices were revealed most dramatically when companies that on paper looked successful, crashed. The profits had been illusory, generated by the accounting policies themselves. Many of those abuses have been stamped out. But even if finance directors play within the rules they can still have an impact on the company's perceived performance.

The financial reporting game is also a tactical one. A company might, for example, anticipate that it is going to have a bad year. It also knows that it has other costs that it could take at any time – perhaps reorganising a factory and making some staff redundant. If it is going to have a bad year anyway, it may be worth taking all the unpleasant expenses at once. Once the pain has been borne that year, next year the results should glow in comparison.

The most common tactic is for companies to try to deliver results that follow a gently rising curve over the years, with neither big rises or falls. City analysts like such a performance, even if they know it's being manipulated. Since the finance director has the public responsibility for delivering the company's results, he will have to attend the company's annual general meeting to hear what the shareholders think. He may be questioned on financial or accounting issues. He will also sit on the board and is answerable to his fellow directors.

Below the finance director, more junior financial accountants do more of the hands-on number crunching. In large companies there will also be accountants responsible for gathering in the results from subsidiaries and feeding them into the group accounts. Management accountants generate the data relevant to the day-to-day running of the business. Some of these roles involve high levels of analysis, looking at ways to improve the profitability of parts of the business. They may involve liaising with the marketing department to develop future marketing strategies.

For there to be any data to analyse at all, someone has to record the company's daily transactions. Accounting technicians have to gather in records of payments to suppliers and receipts from customers, and input those transactions into the financial computer systems. They may have specific responsibilities. There will often be a sales-ledger clerk, responsible for recording details of the company's sales and chasing up slow payers. The purchase-ledger clerk does the same job for purchases that the company makes itself – for example, buying in raw materials. There may be one individual responsible for maintaining records of the company's assets, its furniture, machinery, office equipment, and pool cars. Someone has to organise the payroll, working out what staff are to be paid for that month, or week. There may also be a cashier, responsible for reimbursing expenses, as well as a treasurer with a wider cash-management brief. The treasury role could involve finding the best bank accounts for cash and making sure the company isn't vulnerable to any swings in exchange rates. Individual divisions may have a financial controller or company accountant responsible for the financial reporting and management of that section. Large companies will also have an in-house tax team to consider the tax implications of corporate investments and strategies. Often many of these jobs overlap and their definitions can be vague. Whenever you apply for a job in an accountancy role, make sure you get a full description of exactly what the position involves. An analyst role, for example, may sound exciting but turn out to require little more than tedious number crunching.

If life in different accountancy practices varies with the type of firm, the same is true of life in industry. Consider the multinational with a head office in Reading and subsidiaries in France, Germany and Hong Kong. The finance department will need enough staff to be able to compile the financial reporting data, and the management reporting data, to reflect performance in all locations. There will be several staff at junior grades, reporting up through several management levels until they reach the finance director. A smaller UK company with no overseas subsidiaries will offer a simpler accounting experience. There may be no translations of foreign accounts, for example.

CASE STUDY

Jeremy Tait, aged twenty-nine, completed a degree in Maths and Management at Brunel University and then had to pick a career. He already had work experience to draw on. During his course, he completed three six-month placements with different companies in three very different roles: planning, sales and contracts, and IT marketing. He now works in a financial control position with Marks & Spencer.

I didn't really choose accountancy, accountancy chose me. I wanted a role that was very analytical, but it didn't have to be in finance. I was thinking more of some form of marketing analyst role. But I had an interview for a general management position with food retailer Safeway and met the financial analyst team. Their role seemed to offer what I wanted, so in 1991 I joined Safeway as a systems accountant based in Middlesex and began studying for the Chartered Institute of Management Accountants (CIMA) qualification.

I was free to choose any accountancy qualification but picked CIMA because I preferred its management bias. It covered relevant topics such as marketing and law. The exams were quite a shock at first. It was very different from college and I didn't get a huge amount of study leave. I started doing evening courses but didn't have enough time. So I switched to weekend courses, which were superb. It meant you spent ten weekends a year studying. I quite enjoyed the exams in the end, particularly the final stage.

I stayed about six months as a systems accountant, which was an excellent business introduction. It involved looking at the general ledger and seeing how that linked into other accounting areas. Then I moved to a more strategic finance systems team. Safeway was the first to trial a loyalty card. I looked at ways to encourage customers to spend with us. I found that hard cash was the incentive customers preferred, even though they could have received a greater value of gifts. Safeway was also the first company to introduce 100 per cent scanning at its tills. My role involved finding good uses for all that data. We had lots of product information so we could compare profitability. This was an exciting period for me because we had a blank page to work with. No one knew how much use we could make of the scanning data. But we found many uses. For example, using the demographic information on our customer database, we could look at a geographical area and plan how to tailor a new store to any particular community, assessing which products would do well.

After two and a half years I became a management accountant for the marketing function. I was in charge of all marketing's accounting, including product promotions. I examined issues such as what sort of 'trigger level' we should use. For example, I looked at whether a customer had to spend £4.99 or £5.99 in order to get something in the promotion. I monitored the impact of promotions, whether they achieved their objectives. I built up a database that showed which promotions worked best.

Then in May 1995 I moved to Blockbuster Entertainment as a financial planning analyst. I changed companies largely because Safeway had gone through a strategic review and the role I had been aiming for was made obsolete. I had wanted to move into an operations analysis type role, looking at business systems and improving them. But the consultants had effectively done that work. The only roles really open to me were in financial accounting.

So I joined Blockbuster, which was a completely different type of company. It had only 350 people at head office and was growing massively. I did a lot of marketing analysis, using the skills I had built up at Safeway. I set that role up for Blockbuster – they didn't really do promotional analysis before I went there. I also did the UK stores plan, preparing the financial budgets for the next year, building them up from expected sales and costs. I also looked at bad debts. For example, if someone runs up a fine by returning a video late, but returns it using a drop box, how should Blockbuster chase that debt? If they don't come into the store to rent another video, should we write to them? That could lose goodwill towards the company. But on the other hand, those fines are a valuable source of income. I looked at the options. It was a fascinating job.

After a year, I began looking for another move. Although the company was expanding, it wasn't bringing in new staff under the existing team. My role was expanding but I wasn't getting the kind of promotion I wanted. So in June 1996 I joined Marks & Spencer as finance control manager in the food division. My main role was to see how we could improve profitability. My CIMA training was most useful in this role, where I was performing capital evaluations of promotions. I could dig out the discounted cash-flow concepts I had studied. I understood why you had to cover the capital you spent rather than just look at sales or margins. The work was mentally stimulating, and I worked closely with the buyers, which I enjoyed.

Recently I moved into direct-mail financial control with M&S. Here I am looking at the management accounting and planning for the direct-mail business, a role I haven't done before. I prepare monthly accounts for all the direct-sales areas, such as furniture and flowers. I do the planning and look at marketing initiatives. There are a lot of areas we can look at to improve the financial information we provide. I enjoy adding value to the business. In M&S, they are looking for financial managers who are commercial. They want someone who can combine accounting skills with commercial flair.

I tell young people at M&S that they shouldn't do the CIMA exams unless they are sure they want to go into finance. Once you do accountancy exams, you are stamped as a financial person. So if you really want to go into marketing, you might be better getting a marketing qualification. The problem is, the only way people can decide is through work experience. So I would recommend starting with a general business position and working in different departments, or doing work placements during college like I did.

I have got my options open at the moment. I am now moving into a management accounting role, which means I could look at a financial control position in future. My preferred roles are those where you can have a direct impact on the business.

BANKING AND THE CITY

City accountants have traditionally earned some of the highest salaries. Their image is also distinctive: blue pin-stripe suits are the stereotypical day wear. Many of those who enter the banking and financial service sectors do so after they have gained their qualification elsewhere. Demand for newly qualified staff varies with the general state of the economy. When times are good, the City sector booms. When times turn sour, life becomes less stable. They say investment banks are the first to be hit in a recession, but they are also the first ones to come out of it. But regardless of the financial climate, they will always need internal auditors and people to manage their traders. Since the mid-1990s, job opportunities for accountants in the financial-service organisations have been boosted by concern over regulation.

There is a range of positions for which qualified accountants are suited. Some will be the same as in other types of organisations, such as financial reporting. But accountants within 'product control' will be involved in the accounting that underpins the deals done by traders. The accountants work closely with the traders and will need to make sure that the traders' books balance. Fund-management organisations need accountants to fill equity-analysis roles, posts involving research into particular industry sectors, such as telecommunications, monitoring developments and looking out for investment holdings that should be bought or sold. Risk-management roles involve a type of credit-control work, assessing companies to see if they are safe to do business with. Some accountants work in compliance roles, making sure that the organisation doesn't breach any of the regulations governing its operations. Another option is to go into corporate finance, a high-status area, where accountants look for companies needing growth finance and arrange funding deals. It is very much a matter of personal preference as to which roles are most appealing. A good way to get a feel for all the options is by getting as wide an experience as possible of such clients during an audit training.

The downside to many of these positions is that the hours can be long and antisocial. American investment banks tend to have a reputation for demanding particularly long hours from their staff. However, there are always exceptions and some City and banking roles may be less demanding in terms of time than a life in practice or industry. Despite the high-powered image of these financial-services jobs, recruiters say you don't have to be of the highest calibre to get in. Good management-accounting experience is valued and those who enter the sector need to be willing to learn and to mould to the culture they join.

THE PUBLIC SECTOR

To a certain extent, a public sector accountancy training should differ little from a private-sector training. An NHS trust needs a finance department in the same way as a typical plc does.

The difference stems from the nature of the organisation itself. The key aim of the plc will be to make a decent return for its shareholders. But what about the NHS trust? A key aim will certainly be to create a financially healthy organisation. But what happens when there is a clear argument for increasing numbers of emergency beds and for increasing nurses' pay, but not enough funds to do both? Public-sector life will bring issues of priority, ethics, and judgement to life more starkly than in the private sector. The experience can be a tough one, particularly if the finance team are seen as hacking back costs, the uncaring administrators, when you know you are doing all you can to maximise the use of limited resources. On the positive side, that also means the challenges and achievements can be great too.

Similar arguments apply to local government. The range of tasks could include:

- ensuring IT systems are implemented effectively throughout a local authority
- making sure funds for leisure projects are being allocated to the right projects
- ensuring local taxes are collected properly
- making sure local elected politicians understand the importance of maintaining accurate financial records.

Accountants working in the education sector and within housing associations have to become expert in the particular issues that affect them. The charity sector offers even more choice of environment. The largest charities need significant financial expertise, but even the smaller ones require firm financial control, such as the Edinburgh Festival Theatre Trust which needs a financial manager to control the income from the box office, bars and catering, and maximise the cash available for funding performances.

Apart from jobs within the NHS, local government and the like, there are also careers for people to audit these bodies. The audit of local government and NHS trusts is the responsibility of the Audit Commission, with much of the audit work conducted by its agency, District Audit. The National Audit Office is responsible for auditing central government departments. Both the NAO and District Audit carry out two types of report on the organisations they investigate, financial audit and value-for-money studies.

The traditional financial audit is the public-sector equivalent of the audits conducted by private firms for businesses. Auditors will check the accounts to make sure that the particular organisations' transactions during any year have been correctly recorded. The work involves extra elements. For example, in District Audit, auditors would check that a local authority is correctly claiming any grants to which it is entitled. The audit team would also develop tests to find out whether grants have been used for the right projects, such as money received to pay supply teachers. The tests could include reviewing the county council's personnel and payroll records and talking to relevant schools' headteachers to make sure that teachers have actually been employed.

Value-for-money studies centre around finding ways to improve particular public services, such as the maintenance of council housing or the management of hospital beds. Improving the quality of the service and cutting costs are two key goals. The studies involve interviewing the people who run the service as well as compiling relevant data. For example, a study to maximise the number of hospital beds available could look at how many operations can be conducted on a day-care basis, without overnight hospitalisation. Such a study would involve interviews with surgeons and hospital managers, as well as going through entries in the hospital theatre's register detailing the operations conducted there. Patient stay data, including length of stay and any complications, could be added before the information is analysed for trends, inefficiencies and opportunities for improvement. VFM specialists need to have good interpersonal skills to be able to present findings effectively and persuade managers to accept and act upon recommendations.

Though most people who think about accountancy careers start with the idea of working in industry and practice, and then perhaps focus on tax, there are other related options worth considering. The Inland Revenue needs to train its own staff. This is the other side of the fence to the practice or industry option, but is also a challenging and rewarding one. The Revenue's job is to assess and collect tax from individuals and businesses large and small, collecting around £85 billion a year. Most staff work in local offices around the country, with the rest in specialist offices. Most tax inspectors move into that role from the Revenue's junior ranks, although the Revenue occasionally recruits graduates to train directly as tax inspectors. Apart from tax inspectors, the work of Revenue executives could cover a range of activities, such as managing teams of clerical staff handling taxpayers' affairs. They also handle casework, such as the personal tax affairs of company directors, local businessmen or people with more complicated tax calculations. Compliance officers are responsible for detecting and investigating cases of tax fraud and evasion, while policy and technical specialists advise government ministers on tax policy.

The Revenue runs its own training scheme so staff don't study for a qualification with any of the accountancy bodies. Despite that, experienced tax inspectors are not bound to stay working in the Inland Revenue for ever. Their inside knowledge of the Revenue's thinking and the workings of government is highly prized elsewhere, notably in the accountancy practices which can take that inside knowledge and apply it to their clients' tax returns.

CASE STUDY

Tareque Hossain, aged twenty-six, comes from a family of accountants and so recognised the value in having a professional qualification. He trained with the Chartered Institute of Public Finance and Accountancy while working at Nottingham City Council, qualifying in 1996.

It wasn't a conscious decision to become an accountant, but at the time I graduated in Accounting and Finance at Manchester University in 1993, accountancy seemed to be recognised globally and have prestige. So the next step was to decide the particular accountancy route: chartered, certified or public sector. My decision was influenced by my own personal philosophy. If you are public-service oriented in your philosophy, then the public sector is the way to give something back to the community. In 1993 accountancy was going through a tough time. People were getting laid off in the public sector. I looked at the Milk Round and internal vacancy bulletins and saw this position come up with the City Council as a trainee accountant. I applied, went for an interview and was fortunate enough to get the position.

I had a choice of qualification, but I thought CIPFA was the most relevant. Some people think of CIPFA as the black sheep among the accountancy bodies, but in the public sector I still feel it's a good qualification to have. And it has chartered status, which is what counts.

Accountancy

I studied through a mix of day and block release and didn't find it too bad. The second professional exams were perhaps the toughest. The studying is useful but it doesn't relate directly to real life. It does help to focus the mind on the philosophy behind the public services.

As a trainee, I followed a structured training programme moving between divisions: internal audit, financial planning, financial accounting and financial advice. I worked in each for between six months and a year. The aim is to give you an all-round professional qualification and to give you the skills you need to gain membership. In internal audit you have to check that systems and controls are functioning properly. Financial planning looks at the council's requirements for capital and sources of funding – it's more strategic. Financial accounting concentrates on reporting the council's financial situation.

Now I have moved to become a financial adviser as part of the social-services planning team helping make arrangements for when the council takes over the running of the local social services. The work is very different to the training and to the normal day-to-day work of running the council. I like the variety and it's interesting being part of a planning team. I like the fact there is something tangible that will emerge from our work – we are setting up a new department.

The job has met my expectations in most ways – for example, when you see the streets are being kept clean and you know that, despite working in a time of cuts, the finance department has managed to keep up the service.

I have been here now for four to five years and the idea of a change is not entirely unattractive. I might like a period on the other side, in the private sector, to get a flavour of what it's like. One of the potential disadvantages of the CIPFA qualification is that there isn't so much scope to use it in the private sector, though it is possible to work as a consultant, specialising in public-sector assignments. If people are starting out and deciding on a qualification, I would advise them to think about whether they do want to go into the private sector at some stage. If they do, then the CIPFA qualification may not be the most appropriate.

If I do work in the private sector at some point, I think I would still come back to the public sector in the end because that's where my heart lies. Public service is very worthwhile and I would recommend anyone to go into it.

WORKING ROUTINES

Most accountants will have some kind of cyclical aspect to their work, with the fastest cycles in the industrial environment. Companies generally divide their year into twelve periods which end on a working day somewhere around the end of each month. At the end of each period, management reports are run, detailing sales and purchases, debtor and creditor balances. The accounts team will look out for slow-paying customers and chase them up. The purchase-ledger clerk may have to negotiate with suppliers over disputed invoices. Bank reconciliations are performed to check that the sums the company has in the bank tally with what it thinks should be there. There will be differences, for example, due to cheques that haven't yet cleared. The payroll has to be run in time for staff to be paid when they expect, again often at the end of the month, though some companies work on a thirteen-period basis so the payment date varies through the year.

Higher up the chain, life may stray a bit further from the cyclical pattern, but elements of it remain. The financial director may have to review individual ledgers himself and prepare reports to the Board on the company's performance that month. He is also responsible for strategic issues which can arise at any time. Say the company wants to float on the Stock Exchange. The finance director will need to gather a team of advisers and backers to complete all the legal and financial requirements for the exercise. What if the company needs to update its IT systems following a merger with a US company? The two reporting systems need to be compatible to streamline the preparation of management and financial reports. The finance director may have to call in IT consultants to help. When will be the best time to introduce the system? How much is the company willing to spend? The finance director may have his thoughts interrupted by a call from the auditors asking to fix up a meeting to discuss the planning for this year's audit.

As for the auditors, their cycles tend to be far longer. Generally speaking, most accountancy firms have a busy season stretching from late autumn through to early summer.

Accountancy

Most companies have accounting periods that end on 31 December or 31 March. The auditor can do his planning work before that, but much of the verification of the accounts happens after that close-off date, so things get very busy in midwinter and spring. The summer is traditionally a quiet period when many junior staff study for exams.

CASE STUDY

Karn Hever, aged thirty-one, discovered her interest in an accountancy career by accident. When she left college after completing A levels in English, Maths and Statistics, she didn't know what to do, so started working with her father in the showroom of a used-car dealership.

I showed people round the cars, did basic sales invoicing and passed on all the data to the main office. I helped out on the switchboard and with the typing, but I decided that the bit I liked best was the accounting. So I got a job with the BBC in its accounts department. I started as a cash applications clerk. When cash came in, I had to allocate it to the right accounts. My roles rotated every six months so I also worked on the sales ledger, in credit control, and then on the bought ledger, which recorded purchases, where I became a controller. It was great experience because I had exposure to all these different areas.

After about eighteen months, I wanted to buy a flat and needed more money so I joined General Electric, a US-based company. I worked in a pooled accounting function, handling the inter-company accounts for all GE's businesses. Around this time, I started studying to qualify with the Association of Accounting Technicians after my boss said it would be a good thing for me to do. I attended evening classes two nights a week. GE was good about it – the company paid for my courses, the books and gave me time off to study. The AAT qualification structure was different then, but I got an exemption from the first level because of my A levels, and qualified in 1991. I think the AAT is very good. It gives a thorough grounding and covers things like letter writing and law as well as accounting. Towards the end of my study period, GE depooled its accounting function and so I transferred to one of its business units to help set up an accounting department in Hammersmith, working as an accounts assistant.

After I had been with GE for about four years, I was looking for promotion and so moved to join a Canadian cheese importer, based in Weybridge. I became the company accountant there. Before I joined, the accounts had been prepared by the auditors but the company wanted them brought in-house. So I set everything up. It was a bit scary but fun and each year I had a trip to Canada. While working there I started studying for the Association of Chartered Certified Accountants' qualification. However, the company then decided to make my role more sales oriented and that wasn't what I wanted to do. I helped to recruit my replacement and went to join Racal Electronics as a financial analyst for one of its businesses. I stayed there eighteen months and hated every minute. The job was very boring. I consolidated Racal's figures and sent them to the group accounts department. It was just a number-crunching role using bits of software. I also found the culture very old school.

About six months ago I found a new job with an international firm of architects as a project accountant. I still have to finish my second year with the ACCA. Studying is hard. Since my time at General Electric I have generally been the main person responsible for the office, so I could never guarantee to leave work on time. For me, I think that studying at home in my own time is probably better. Colleges can be inflexible and the classes large.

My advice to people starting out in accountancy would be that you are better off going for a large company first. You will have more chance to move around and try out different areas. You should also go for a company that definitely gives you study leave. Companies often say they have a study package but they may simply mean they let you go home half an hour early. A good company will give you two weeks' study leave, otherwise your studying eats into your holidays. Studying is boring. Half of it you never use and the sheer volume of material can be daunting. But if you have a qualification you can earn more, and as soon as you are part-qualified you can apply for many more jobs.

I have enjoyed almost all my accounting jobs and got a lot of satisfaction from them. Every time I have changed, I have gone into something different. I enjoy what I do. And if you have a qualification, there is a lot of work out there.

2 Breaking In

If you asked a hundred people what it takes to be an accountant, you can bet all of them would say you had to be good with numbers. That is certainly true, particularly in more junior roles and earlier in careers, before more general management and strategic skills become increasingly important. If you really can't add up or go into a cold sweat at the sight of a column of figures, then start looking for another career right away. However, numerical ability isn't enough. There are many other attributes required of the aspiring accountant.

PERSONAL QUALITIES

This is what the Institute of Chartered Accountants in England & Wales, the largest UK accountancy body, says a chartered accountant needs to be:

- a good communicator
- a high academic achiever
- a good team player
- comfortable in a numerate environment
- able to manage time effectively
- analytical
- self-motivated.

Notice that being 'comfortable in a numerate environment' comes fourth on the list. First place goes to communication skills, vital in many careers these days, with accountancy being no exception: for the auditor who has to explain to a client why he thinks there is a problem in the number of late-paying customers; or the management accountant writing a report that proposes to tighten the budget for next year; or the finance director telling his company's board about last year's financial performance; or the purchase-ledger clerk explaining to a supplier why his bill hasn't been paid yet.

Academic ability is most important for anyone wanting to train for a qualification with one of the major accountancy bodies. If you are bad at exams and hate studying then you can still find a role in accounts administration, but you have to be prepared not to achieve the highest promotions. People can reach responsible positions without any accounting qualification at all, but they are the exceptions to the rule.

Accountants are often found working within teams of people. An audit team will include staff of different levels of experience, but to operate smoothly all members need to work together. A company's finance department may include a payroll clerk, one or more sales-ledger clerks, purchase-ledger clerks, management accountants and reporting accountants. Add in the finance director and the treasury department and you end up with large numbers of people who have to co-ordinate their activities to keep the company on the financial rails. If you can't get on with other people, you will find life hard. Even if you run your own practice, theoretically working alone, you still have to get on with clients.

Time management is one of those general skills that everyone in the commercial environment needs to develop. Accountants often find themselves working against the clock. In practice firms, staff and partners have to keep records of their time so that the firm can bill clients accurately. Tax specialists often have to fill out forms which show what they have been doing for each six-minute period of every working day. For clients, time is literally money and trainees can find the pressure to perform at speed stressful. In corporate departments accountants often have to produce reports at short notice or process a certain number of transactions to a weekly or monthly deadline. Don't expect fellow staff to be sympathetic if you have to pay them late because you couldn't get the payroll data processed on time.

Analytical ability is one of the accountant's core skills. Figures are just the raw data used to record corporate performance or determine management decisions. Analysing those figures to draw conclusions about the past or future is a vital part of many accountants' work. Auditors perform analysis to spot errors in reporting. Forensic accountants analyse data to find evidence of fraud or false accounting. Management accountants adjust budgets and targets to achieve optimum performance. Financial analysts in the City compare a company's performance against others in the sector to see whether it's a sound investment prospect.

While team spirit is important, accountants have to be self-motivated, particularly if they want to study for professional qualifications. If you can't discipline yourself to go and read an accountancy textbook, you will struggle. You may also have to work long hours in deserted offices late into the evening.

The list of attributes required by accountants needn't stop here. Business sense is important even to those accountants who choose to work in audit. How can you advise clients on their businesses if you don't understand them? And given that accountants spend their life working with money, on paper at least, employers will look out for signs of personal integrity. People who work in financial posts need to be above suspicion of fraudulent activity. If you are attracted by the public sector, on top of all the other attributes expected of you, you will probably need to demonstrate genuine interest in the area. Why are you particularly concerned that the NHS is run efficiently? You will also need to show an understanding of the particular stresses that come with the sector.

LEVELS OF ENTRY

You can start out on an accountancy career at several levels and with a variety of qualifications. There are openings for school leavers, for graduates, and for postgraduate students. There are also opportunities for mature entrants who have done something else first, then decided they want a professional qualification. However, these people are a small minority of the total. Promotion and responsibility will come faster if you start at graduate level, rather than straight after school. Some professional bodies, such as the Institute of Chartered Accountants of Scotland, allow only graduates to study for their qualification.

Not everyone, of course, is looking for rapid promotion. If you are looking for a stable job in an accounts department, perhaps running the sales ledger or administering the payroll, then there is no need to get a degree. You can join a company straight from school if you want and work your way up, gaining experience and professional qualifications as you go. Most of the jobs will be in the data-processing side of the finance department, and there are more options for school leavers in industry and commerce, though some accountancy firms, such as KPMG, do now take on staff at this level.

Graduates have a wider range of accounting-job options open to them and the full range of professional qualifications from which to choose. Graduate training programmes are run by employers in public practice, industry, and the public sector, so gaining a degree keeps all the options open. Your degree doesn't need to be related to finance at all. Employers don't expect their accounting trainees to have studied accountancy before. Research over the years has even shown that people who studied accountancy at university don't achieve the highest pass rates in their professional exams. This could be because accountancy graduates become complacent about the professional exams they have to take. Mathematics graduates generally do best and engineers have also traditionally done well. However, English graduates also regularly make the grade. Regardless of your degree subject, you will need to convince your prospective employer that you have a genuine interest in business. If the interviewer thinks you really want to spend your life writing poetry, he may prefer to employ someone with a proven business sense. Any evidence of business experience that you can show, even making a profit on a student newspaper, for example, will help your job prospects.

Postgraduates are a special case and definitely improve their chances of employment by concentrating on a business-related topic. Nevertheless, KPMG says that if you have the qualities they seek, a business head, good communication skills and strong analytical ability, for example, a postgraduate degree in Serbian rock formations would not rule you out of contention for a training contract.

Most accountancy qualifications take at least three years of juggling study and work. As outside commitments increase, say through family and children, achieving the balancing act between home and career can only get harder. Some firms may be interested in older applicants, but for consultancy roles rather than accounting. You will need to have some fairly extensive expertise or skill that the firm needs and that fits in with its existing activities. For example, the largest firms have a head-hunting service within their management consultancy divisions. Clearly, if you have human resources or recruitment experience and join one of the firms you won't be pushed towards an accounting career, but you will be expected to fit in with the culture of a firm with strong accounting and audit roots.

SIMPLIFYING THE DECISION PROCESS

Once you have formed the general impression that you are interested in a career as an accountant, you still face a number of tough career decisions. What sector should you train in and what qualification should you gain? There are numerous bodies offering qualifications and you can work in any sector of the economy. It all seems very confusing and it can be unless you adopt a structured approach to your career decision.

There are four key decisions to make when starting out on your career in accountancy:

1. What kind of role do you want?
2. What environment do you want to work in?
3. What kind of qualification are you looking for?
4. Which employers provide the best opportunities given your ambitions?

The answer to one question may affect another. For example, most trainees in the big accountancy firms sit exams set by the English and Welsh, Scottish or Irish chartered institutes. Accountants in the public sector have traditionally trained for a qualification with the Chartered Institute of Public Finance and Accountancy, although this assumption is now weakening. Many accountants who know they want to work in industry train with the Chartered Institute of Management Accountants. These aren't rigid rules, however. Some industry trainees opt for the English and Welsh, Scottish and Irish chartered institutes, and some big firms train staff with other professional bodies, such as CIMA, CIPFA or the Association of Chartered Certified Accountants, which has become increasingly popular among smaller firms.

WHAT KIND OF ROLE DO YOU WANT?

Do you want to be generating the accounts for an organisation, or reviewing those accounts? Would you rather be based within a company, perhaps having the chance to work on strategic projects? Or would you see yourself as good at developing relations with others, where having a portfolio of clients would prove satisfying? The first of these options would suggest opting for a management accounting role, while the latter suggests public practice might be more suitable. You should also consider whether it is straight accounting that appeals, or whether you might want to concentrate on a tax career. If you are interested in tax you could train in practice, industry or opt for a government body such as the Inland Revenue.

WHAT ENVIRONMENT DO YOU WANT TO WORK IN?

Would you relish the extra moral and ethical issues that may crop up during a career in the public sector? Or is the generation of profits more exciting? The gap between the public and private sectors has closed in terms of the accounting rules applied, but there are still strong cultural differences.

WHAT KIND OF QUALIFICATION ARE YOU LOOKING FOR?

Partly, this decision will be determined by the level at which you start your accountancy career, whether after school or at graduate level. If you are a school leaver, you can't train with the Scottish institute, for example. As mentioned above, some bodies are associated with particular branches of accounting. There are also differences in subject matter and the time period allowed to qualify. You need to study the options with each professional body carefully to make sure your choice suits you.

WHICH EMPLOYERS PROVIDE THE BEST OPPORTUNITIES?

Do you want a large employer, perhaps with international links? Or would a smaller, potentially friendlier, environment make you happier? What training support do the employers provide? Do they encourage staff to study for professional qualifications? How are they considered in their industry sector? What qualifications do the finance director and other staff have? Will they respect the qualification that you want to gain? Some of this information you can learn from company brochures or careers advisers. Some you may have to find out by asking direct questions at the job-interview stage.

THE QUALIFICATION MAZE

Deciding on your preferred role and environment is likely to be the easiest part. Choosing a qualification can be a different matter. The accountancy profession is characterised by what seems at first sight a bewildering range of bodies with impressive titles offering their own qualifications.

For those looking for a traditional accountancy training, without going straight for a specialisation such as tax, most prestige attaches to the six organisations making up a group known as the Consultative Committee of Accountancy Bodies (CCAB). These are as follows:

>   Association of Chartered Certified Accountants (ACCA)

Chartered Institute of Management Accountants (CIMA)

Chartered Institute of Public Finance and Accountancy (CIPFA)

Institute of Chartered Accountants in England & Wales (ICAEW)

Institute of Chartered Accountants in Ireland (ICAI)

Institute of Chartered Accountants of Scotland (ICAS)

Accountants who gain one of these qualifications possess a valuable commodity. Achieving membership is known to require ability in digesting and displaying theoretical knowledge, but members of these bodies have also had to prove themselves in the workplace. Another body worth mentioning here is the Association of Accounting Technicians (AAT), which recruiting specialists regard as a para-professional qualification. The AAT qualification is aimed at school leavers rather than graduates and is well regarded in industry and practice. Once you have the AAT qualification you can always go on to gain a further qualification, perhaps that offered by CIMA if you work in industry, or the ACCA if you work in practice.

Of course, it isn't necessary to gain any accountancy qualification at all. Having a proven track record of work experience in a financial department, building up expertise with, say, payroll and the sales ledger and mastering a number of different accounting and IT packages should be enough to allow you to move around different companies. You can also enhance your marketability by building up experience with a particular type of business, and its accounting peculiarities. But it is as true of accountancy as of any other profession that employers like to see qualifications on the CV. If things get tight, if the economy falters and potential employees outnumber jobs available, people with both paper qualifications and work experience will get an interview ahead of someone with only work experience.

Non-graduates who have worked for some time in a financial role and want to skip over the AAT qualification to take another with higher entry requirements, such as CIMA, may be able to do so since some institutes will accept mature applicants with work-based experience but without the necessary academic qualification.

Since the choice of your professional body is so important, it's worth spending some time looking at the particular characteristics of each.

ASSOCIATION OF CHARTERED CERTIFIED ACCOUNTANTS

ACCA members only won the right to call themselves 'Chartered Certified Accountants' in 1996 when the Privy Council gave its assent after a long campaign. Having that 'chartered' title is an important status symbol in the accountancy profession, which is characterised by the strong rivalry between the leading institutes.

The ACCA has around 60,000 members and 130,000 students around the world, with approximately half its members and 55 per cent of students based overseas. Women make up 20 per cent of UK membership and 31 per cent of overseas members. The ACCA is growing fast internationally and is unique amongst the UK accountancy bodies in that it offers an option for students to be examined on International Accounting Standards, rather than UK standards. This option is not recommended for typical UK students, since the UK has its own accounting rules, but it could be helpful to anyone working in a country which does use the international equivalents.

The ACCA is highly flexible in the ways it allows students to gain its qualification. Students can study full-time and pass all the Association's exams before gaining any practical experience, or they can take the more common approach and study for the exams while holding down a job. Day-release, evening class, distance learning and open access study methods are available.

Again, the ACCA qualification is flexible in that members are not associated with any particular field of accountancy. Of the Association's 30,000 UK members, around 9,000 work in practice, 13,000 in commerce and industry and the rest in central and local government, the health sector, education, public services and utilities.

The ACCA has also launched a new lower-level qualification after withdrawing its backing for the widely respected Association of Accounting Technicians. The ACCA's own rival technician-level qualification is primarily exam based, whereas the AAT's is essentially experience based. The ACCA said the move would be helpful to overseas students since it was difficult to transfer and monitor the AAT's system of work-based assessments overseas. The new technician qualification does seem to be gaining support abroad.

CHARTERED INSTITUTE OF MANAGEMENT ACCOUNTANTS

CIMA has a world-wide membership totalling 45,000, with 33,000 of those in the UK. It has a large number of students, with approximately 36,000 training in the UK, and another 23,000 training abroad. The institute is enjoying a growth phase with its membership total rising by 7 per cent in 1996. Student numbers also continue to expand at an even larger rate. Women make up an increasing share of the membership, up to around 15 per cent compared with just 8 per cent five years ago.

CIMA members are traditionally associated with careers in industry, but they also work in the public sector, in the NHS and local councils, education and the arts, and are increasingly employed in accountancy firms in consultancy roles.

CIMA is expanding its international base, with offices outside the UK as far-flung as Sri Lanka. CIMA's 1997 President was based in Hong Kong. The institute also has plans to start training CIMA students in China.

CHARTERED INSTITUTE OF PUBLIC FINANCE AND ACCOUNTANCY

CIPFA is the traditional professional body for accountants in the public sector. Almost half CIPFA's 13,000 members work in local government, around 14 per cent in the health sector, while smaller percentages work in public bodies and central government, education, housing associations and charities, and regulated utilities such as water, gas and electricity. At most 10 per cent of CIPFA members work in the private sector. About a quarter of the membership are women.

Student numbers have been falling in the late 1990s, in part because public-sector trainee accountants now have much more freedom to choose their preferred accountancy qualification, rather than being automatically pushed towards CIPFA. The ACCA and CIMA appear to have been benefiting at CIPFA's expense, attracting increasing numbers of students in central and local government and in the NHS. CIPFA's falling student numbers, compounded by financial problems, have triggered rumours that the institute could be forced to merge with one of the other CCAB bodies.

INSTITUTE OF CHARTERED ACCOUNTANTS IN ENGLAND & WALES

The ICAEW has over 111,500 members, with over 10,700 student accountants registered on training contracts. The proportion of those trainees who are graduates has crept steadily upwards and now sits at over 94 per cent. By 1997, women made up 16.6 per cent of the membership, but 36.4 per cent of the trainees, reflecting the gradual shift in the sexual make-up of the profession as the proportion of women entering it rises. The vast majority of trainees work in public practice, employed by a firm of chartered accountants. Approved training offices range from the giants in the field, the so-called Big Five firms, down to small, single-office firms. The institute also runs the TOPP scheme, Training Outside Public Practice, which allows its trainees to work in industry or commerce. The ICAEW claims that around 25 per cent of the top 500 companies in the UK have a chartered accountant as their chairman or managing director. High-profile chartered accountants include Sir Brian Jenkins, once head of Coopers & Lybrand before its merger and a former Mayor of London, now chairman of the Woolwich. Sir Paul Girolami, the former chairman of Glaxo (prior to the formation of Glaxo Wellcome), is also an ACA.

The ICAEW has an internationally spread membership, with over 13 per cent of its members working overseas, particularly in the USA, Australia, Canada and Hong Kong. Though many of these will have qualified in the UK and moved abroad for a few years' international experience, there are now registered training offices in four countries outside the UK: Cyprus, Malaysia, Singapore and Malta. More may be recognised in future in Eastern Europe, the Middle East and East Africa. The qualification is recognised widely abroad, in all Commonwealth countries, Canada, Australia and New Zealand, in many US states and across Europe.

The institute has a section in its web site designed to explain in simple terms the various careers available in chartered accountancy. It's worth having a browse to get a flavour of what ACAs do, and also the character of the institute. You can find the site at www.icaew.co.uk

INSTITUTE OF CHARTERED ACCOUNTANTS IN IRELAND

The institute celebrated its centenary in 1988 and now has a membership of just over 10,100, of whom over three quarters work in either Northern Ireland or the Republic of Ireland. There are about 2,200 students in training. Though most students train in public practice firms, some do gain the qualification while working in industry.

INSTITUTE OF CHARTERED ACCOUNTANTS OF SCOTLAND

ICAS is the only UK accountancy institute which teaches all its students as well as examining them. It is also unique in that it only accepts graduates to train for membership. ICAS has around 14,100 members, and almost 1,500 students. Although clearly the favourite body among Scottish accountants, ICAS maintains an international outlook, and is increasingly involved in the development of accounting practice in Eastern Europe.

Around 47 per cent of the membership work in industry

and commerce. Almost one in five members are female. ICAS has an option for aspiring CAs who want to train in industry, known as training 'Outwith Public Practice'. Trainees in 'authorised' organisations train for ICAS membership while gaining practical experience in their chosen industry sector. The Scottish institute has also been considering whether it should offer a more junior, technician-level qualification.

ASSOCIATION OF ACCOUNTING TECHNICIANS

The AAT was set up in 1980 by five of the main UK accountancy bodies (ACCA, CIMA, CIPFA, ICAEW, ICAS) to provide a qualification and a membership body for skilled accounting staff employed in industry and commerce, practice or the public sector. It recognises the skills of the accounting technicians who may, if they choose, go on to study for the qualification of one of the sponsoring bodies. The qualification is essentially experience based rather than exam based. The AAT now has around 25,500 full members and 52,000 student members. As mentioned above, the ACCA no longer supports the AAT but has set up its own technician-level qualification.

OTHER ACCOUNTANCY BODIES

Though you might think that the different professional bodies named so far allow enough choice to anyone wanting an accountancy career, there are more. For example, you could choose to join the Institute of Company Accountants (IComA), Institute of Cost and Executive Accountants (ICEA), Institute of Financial Accountants (IFA), or the International Association of Book-keepers (IAB).

Though members of these bodies may achieve high professional standards and be well-regarded by their employers, it has to be said that membership does not carry the status that comes from membership of one of the CCAB bodies. Jeff Grout, managing director of accountancy recruitment specialists Robert Half, says: 'In some cases there is no name awareness at all in the job market-place, and in other cases, they are seen as second-rate qualifications. CCAB qualifieds are almost always employable and have a passport to move between jobs.' Anyone starting out on an accountancy career should remember that, even if you work hard to qualify, it's the attitude of the job market that makes the studying worthwhile.

INSTITUTE OF COMPANY ACCOUNTANTS

The IComA has around 5,000 UK members and 1,500 students, with a further 1,000 members and 1,000 students overseas. It has emerged over the years from the merger of an assortment of similar accountancy bodies and adopted its present title in September 1990. Members work in a wide range of business and non-commercial organisations in accounting and managerial positions of varying levels. Public-practice members specialise in providing accountancy services to small businesses. Members style themselves Incorporated Company Accountant.

INSTITUTE OF COST AND EXECUTIVE ACCOUNTANTS

The ICEA was incorporated in 1958 and describes itself as the 'second biggest cost accounting body in the United Kingdom'. It has fifteen UK branches and eighteen overseas branches, with a total of around 3,600 members and about 2,000 registered students. Members work in companies large and small and in local authorities and in a range of roles including accounting, costing, internal auditing, financial decision-making and taxation. Members can call themselves Incorporated Executive Accountants.

INSTITUTE OF FINANCIAL ACCOUNTANTS

The IFA was established in 1916 and offers an accounting qualification to accountants working in industry and commerce. It currently has around 8,000 members and 11,000 students. Members hold company positions such as company accountant, chief accountant and financial director. They must have demonstrated their knowledge and ability to handle the financial management of a business, either through examinations or by an independent assessment of their competence. Members use the title Incorporated Financial Accountant.

INTERNATIONAL ASSOCIATION OF BOOK-KEEPERS

The International Association of Book-keepers represents bookkeepers in commerce and industry around the world. It offers a professional qualification in bookkeeping, leading to membership. It requires no formal educational entry requirements and encourages people of any age to study for its qualification. It also offers stand-alone diplomas in computerised bookkeeping, payroll administration and small business financial management.

SPECIALIST QUALIFICATIONS

The vast majority of people who call themselves accountants gain a qualification with one of the bodies already mentioned. However, there are yet more options. If you are absolutely sure that you want to become a tax adviser, for example, there isn't really a need for you to follow the accountancy entry route. You could go straight for a specialist tax qualification. If you want to work in a company's treasury department you could focus on gaining a qualification with the Association of Corporate Treasurers. It's worth considering these specialist options, although most who opt for them will already have gained some other more general accounting qualification first.

CHARTERED INSTITUTE OF TAXATION

The CIoT is the key professional body for tax specialists. Its exams are notoriously hard to pass – it is rare for the proportion of students that do pass at any sitting to cross the 50 per cent line. For that reason, membership conveys considerable status. Though not essential for everyone embarking on a tax career, membership may help career prospects. Members have traditionally included many qualified accountants and lawyers, though now some Big-Five firms are recruiting staff to study immediately for the CIoT exams. There are two levels of membership. Associates earn the right to use the letters ATII, while Fellows use the letters FTII. Candidates can study for the normal tax exams, or opt for a VAT specialist route.

ASSOCIATION OF TAXATION TECHNICIANS

The ATT is sponsored by the Chartered Institute of Taxation and since its formation in 1989 has attracted around 2,400 members and 3,500 students. The qualification is aimed at junior tax specialists in industry, commerce, the public sector and professional practices. Members call themselves Taxation Technicians and can use their qualification as a stepping stone to membership of the CIoT, using it to qualify for registration as a candidate for the CIoT's ATII exam.

ASSOCIATION OF CORPORATE TREASURERS

The ACT was set up in 1979 and is dedicated to the education and training of those involved in finance and treasury management, defined as the efficient management of liquidity and financial risk in a business. Not all the ACT's members actually work as treasurers – over one fifth are finance directors. Others hold posts as managing directors, chief executives and chairmen. Many of those who take the qualification have already qualified as chartered accountants and specialised in the treasury function. It is also common for lawyers, tax specialists and corporate finance analysts to seek membership.

INSOLVENCY PRACTITIONERS ASSOCIATION

The IPA was founded in 1961 as a discussion group for accountants who specialised in insolvency. It became incorporated under its current name in 1973 and introduced its first exams for membership in 1981, though no one actually managed to pass until 1983. The Association is empowered by the Insolvency Act 1986 to grant and renew insolvency licences as a means of regulating the insolvency profession. In 1989 the Association's exams became the basis for the specialist exams set by the Joint Insolvency Examinations Board, now the primary qualification for insolvency practitioners. The JIEB exams are notoriously hard. You don't have to be an accountant to sit them, though many accountants do once they decide to specialise in the insolvency field.

More recently, the IPA recognised that there was no qualification for those working in more junior positions in the insolvency field who didn't need to apply for a licence to run insolvency appointments themselves. As a result the IPA introduced a Certificate of Proficiency in Insolvency, less arduous than the JIEB papers, but providing a recognised qualification for insolvency specialists.

YOUR FIRST EMPLOYER

Once you have decided to train as an accountant in practice, you then have to decide which kind of firm to join. One of the key factors to consider is how big, or small, you want the firm to be.

The top end of the audit and accounting market has become increasingly dominated by a small number of giant audit firms. The group, known as the Big Five, includes Arthur Andersen, Deloitte & Touche, Ernst & Young, KPMG, and PricewaterhouseCoopers. This firm, known familiarly as PwC, was formed in July 1998 from the merger of two Big Six practices – Coopers & Lybrand and Price Waterhouse. PwC is a giant organisation, earning global revenue of over $15.3bn for its 1998 financial year. The Big Five form a coherent group in the UK in that there is clear water between the size of their fees and those of the trailing pack. Coopers alone recorded gross UK fees of £766m in 1996/97. BDO Stoy Hayward, then eighth-ranking UK firm, earned gross fees of just over £106m in the year to March 1997. Most firms outside the top ten earn fees well below £100m and fees for firms ranked thirty-plus by size will be somewhere between

£5m and £10m. Yet these medium-sized firms are still way ahead of their several hundred smaller rivals, the vast majority of which earn fees under £1m a year.

The Big Five have a stranglehold on the audits of the UK's largest companies. Ten years ago, the leading group consisted of eight firms (including Binder Hamlyn, now with Arthur Andersen, and Arthur Young, now part of Ernst & Young). The Big Eight audited 78.8 per cent of the *Times* 1000, with medium-sized firms auditing 11.1 per cent. By 1996, as the Big Six, those firms had increased their share to 91.9 per cent of the market. PricewaterhouseCoopers alone now audits almost half of the UK's top 100 companies, more than any other firm.

The Big Five continue to expand in staffing terms too and have a huge demand for graduate trainees. PwC takes on about 1,500 graduate trainees a year, while KPMG takes 500 to 600, though at the peak of the booming late eighties in one year 1,000 recruits signed on to train with the firm. Ernst & Young and Deloittes take 400 plus, and Arthur Andersen 350. These figures jump around each year as the economy or the firms' own requirements change, but it is clear that the large accountancy firms train the vast majority of the UK's chartered accountants. About 90 per cent of KPMG's new joiners have a 2.1 or above, and around one in twenty applicants receives a job offer with the firm. The selection process has also been developed to get as true a picture as possible of the individual's potential to succeed with the firm. Candidates attend an assessment centre where they are required to complete a range of activities, including an in-tray exercise and group meetings. An in-tray exercise is designed to test a candidate's efficiency in dealing with letters, reports, and all the other mass of information that could pile up on an employee's desk. The recruiter is looking for the ability to prioritise items in order of importance so that urgent items are dealt with first. Time pressure will be applied, so the trick is to skim through the lot quickly, sorting as you go. Common sense should tell you that if you get engrossed reading the first item, a long but unimportant message from an imaginary colleague, you won't impress.

David Miller, national graduate recruitment partner at KPMG, says: 'Academic thinking is taken for granted. Our selection process is all about trying to find people with the right mix of skills – client responsiveness, thinking skills, business skills. We are looking for personal effectiveness, for dynamic people who can cope with multi tasks, management skills, team skills, team leadership skills. A few years ago we wouldn't particularly have been testing people's interest in business but nowadays we focus very strongly on that. We believe that unless you are interested in business, this isn't the right career to be going into.'

Audit remains the main division taking new recruits, though some do go straight into tax, corporate recovery (insolvency), and information risk management, the modern name for computer audit. A few may get the chance to go into corporate finance and consultancy. Trends do affect the firms, however. Recently, tax consulting has become one of the most competitive battlegrounds between the firms, creating more vacancies for graduates to go straight into a tax position.

Graduate trainees are taken on by the firms on a fairly standard open-ended employment contract. Alongside the contract with the firm, trainee accountants also have to register with the particular professional body with which they hope to qualify. The firms commit themselves to a high level of support designed to get their trainees through that body's professional exams. They pay salaries while staff attend full-time exam courses, some of which last for two to three months at a time, as well as stumping up for exam fees and the cost of tuition. The aim is to get staff through the exams at the first attempt. If you fail first time round, most firms will probably expect you to pay for the second set of exam fees and revision courses, which may need to be taken during holiday allowances. If you fail twice, most firms retain the right to terminate your employment contract, though if you have worked well in the job itself and business is booming, they may still keep you on. How tough they are on this point varies, so before you accept a training contract you might want to find out your potential employer's likely attitude, though subtly. It is probably better to ask a junior staff member rather than an interviewing partner, so as not to give the impression you expect to have problems with the exams. Firms usually give candidates the chance to talk informally to staff outside the interview room, and you should make the most of this opportunity.

Most trainees study for membership of the ICAEW if in England or Wales, or for membership of ICAS in Scotland and ICAI in Ireland. These are the traditional audit-based qualifications, but they are no longer the only options. New entrants to KPMG's public-sector division have the option to qualify with CIPFA. In Arthur Andersen's corporate financial services division, which includes insolvency and corporate finance work, new joiners have the option to train for the ACCA qualification. At Andersens and KPMG, tax entrants can also go straight for a tax qualification rather than gaining an ACA first, as was common in the past. KPMG now runs a 'tax business school' where entrants enter a full-time technical training programme for nine months during which they take the exams of the CIoT. Assuming they pass, for the rest of their training contract they just concentrate on building up practical tax experience. In the past, tax specialists generally did their chartered accountancy qualification first, then went on to do the CIoT exams, and this remains an option in most firms.

You should also ask any potential training firm about the training support it provides, opportunities to work on different types of client, the potential to move between departments, including insolvency and corporate recovery, and the potential for overseas work, if that interests you. Try to establish how the firm is perceived in the outside world and remember that to some extent where you start impacts on your next move. It will be much harder to move from a one-partner firm to the Big Five after qualification than to move there from a medium-sized firm. Similarly, though the middle-tier firms are generally pleased to take in staff from the Big Five, if you move too far down the size scale, your experience will not be relevant. If you have only audited listed clients, such as Cadbury Schweppes or British Aerospace, how will you understand that a self-employed businessman may want more counselling and psychological support rather than purely technical advice? It is probably best for most people to keep their options open as far as possible. Decide on your own priorities and then try to match them against the packages the firms offer.

As far as geography is concerned, London will offer the best banking assignments due to its position as an international financial centre. It is also probably true that the further away from the capital you get, the fewer plc audits you are likely to encounter. But beyond that, the range of work experience should be pretty similar. Salaries may vary slightly to take account of the expense of living in the capital.

Though the vast majority of new staff joining the audit firms are graduates, there is some demand for school leavers. KPMG, for example, takes about twenty people into its London office, while offices around the country take in smaller numbers. Before its merger with Price Waterhouse, Coopers & Lybrand alone took in around fifty to one hundred people across the UK. Deloitte & Touche, however, employs school leavers very rarely. In general, the number of places available is far smaller than for graduates, but may grow as the firms review their working practices. Firms are realising that there is some basic audit work that doesn't need to be done by the more expensive graduates. In Coopers, school leavers were able to progress to manager level within the firm's human resources advisory practice, working on expatriate tax clients, for example. School-leaver entrants had the option to study for the AAT qualifications. Those that did well enough could then go on to study for another qualification, often with the ACCA. Though a useful option for those who really don't want to go on to further education, joining as a school leaver clearly does cut down the choice of qualifications available.

Another example of experimentation by the firms was the elite scheme introduced by Coopers prior to its merger. Under this scheme, twenty graduates from five universities around the world trained in a country other than where they studied. The twenty were marked out from the start as high fliers and the programme aimed to strengthen international links within the firm. Although unclear whether the scheme would be continued in the same form following the merger of Coopers and Price Waterhouse, it serves as an innovative example of the increasing keenness among leading firms to attract top candidates who can themselves help to develop global practices.

Despite training a vast majority of tomorrow's accountants in practice, the Big Five don't train them all. There are many medium and small firms who take in some trainees each year. There are also many certified firms, as well as the traditional ICAEW or ICAS or ICAI dominated firms. It is very much a matter of personal choice where you decide to train. The largest firms offer the largest clients. That means you can work on household-name companies, but will be a smaller cog and probably work on a smaller range of clients since each large assignment will last longer than would a small audit. If you are more attracted by owner-managed businesses, you should look for a firm that promotes itself as a specialist in that area. If you want to progress to a City job, find a firm with City clients, be it large or medium-sized. Another point to note is that the largest firms are increasingly organised along industry lines – that means you may be assigned to a particular sector, say banking, and then spend most of your training contract working with clients in that sector. On the positive side, that allows you to develop an in-depth understanding of that sector, which will be valued highly by the firm, by clients, and by potential employers in the sector. On the downside, it may trap you in that sector when you would have discovered a greater affinity with retailing had you had a chance to work with such clients. There is something to be said for the more generalist experience which used to be far more common, where a trainee might work on a bank's accounts one week and a travel agent's the next. Small firms will be more likely to offer this kind of variety.

The final, but perhaps most important, factor is whether you get on with the people already there. Believe it or not, there do seem to be subtle differences in the types of personalities attracted to different practices, so find a group that suits you.

Once qualified, career opportunities with firms depend on

the usual factors: personal ability, the demand for people with your particular skills, and the success of the firm to maintain and develop its business. It's hard to see that far ahead when you join, but if you do well in the actual work and gain your target qualification, you should expect a healthy career path. And if your first firm doesn't meet your expectations, you can always move to another once you have proved your ability. Firms expect a large proportion of their newly qualified accountants to leave for business jobs.

INDUSTRY

Choosing an employer in industry involves pretty much the same criteria for an aspiring accountant as for someone entering any other management discipline. The name of the company you join, and the reputation it has within the business community, will impact on your later career moves. Probably no one will know how good the training you had really was, or how wide the breadth of experience you gained, but a blue-chip name will open doors. Companies such as Mars, Unilever, Procter & Gamble, Marks & Spencer, and the oil giants such as Shell will attract high-quality graduates. In general, work experience with any one of the FTSE 100 companies will have a positive impact on your CV.

Having said that, the training you receive in your first job will determine your confidence and ability to progress to posts of higher responsibility, so you should research the kind of exam support the different companies give to accountants studying for the different accountancy qualifications. For example, CIMA runs two levels of grading for approved training companies. The top grade shows a high level of commitment from the employer, while the general one offers basic comfort that the support is there. If you want a particular qualification, perhaps an ACA rather than CIMA, you need to find a company supportive of that approach. Beyond the straight accountancy training, you need to build up management skills as soon as possible. The best companies will train staff in IT and communication skills too.

Pharmaceuticals giant Glaxo Wellcome puts its finance trainees through the CIMA exams. The trainees cover the basics by attending evening courses but get study leave for revision courses and the exams themselves. Glaxo will pay for resits, though the company claims that failure is rare and third attempts virtually unheard of. Personalised training programmes are drawn up for each recruit to develop any particular areas of weakness, for example in computer skills or interpersonal issues such as conflict resolution or how to make effective presentations. Asda also lines its graduate recruits up for the CIMA exams. Again, trainees do most studying in their own time, in this case on Saturday mornings at a recommended training college, and study leave is limited to the exam period. The company expects its recruits to pass their accountancy exams first time. Anyone who doesn't has to explain themselves. The company's attitude depends on whether individuals are thought to be pulling their weight, so no general rule for the outcome can be given. There is considerable other in-house training, covering the usual areas such as IT and interpersonal skills.

When choosing between the different trainee packages, examine closely the type of work you will be performing. Is it all number crunching or does it allow for some analytical work? Will you get pigeon-holed in a particular role, such as financial reporting, or are there opportunities to try your hand at different activities within the finance function? And though you may not want to stay with your first employer for long beyond qualification, it is worth looking at the potential for career advancement. Does the company have a track record of promoting its staff? If it is a multinational, can you move around different group companies? Do staff have the chance to work at subsidiaries or offices overseas, for a few months or even a few years?

Of course, you may not want to work in a FTSE 100 company or a multinational. This is another choice you need to consider, because where you start will influence your future career path. Employers tend to prefer candidates who have worked in companies or industries similar to their own. So if you start in a small, family-owned business, Blue Chip plc will be less keen to employ you than if you had worked for Rival plc. Similarly, if you are most interested in the small-business sector, then that will be the most relevant place to start your career.

With so many companies and potential employers to choose from, narrow the range by thinking about the sector that interests you most. Retailing is one of the most popular areas, along with 'fmcg', otherwise known as fast-moving consumer goods.

PUBLIC SECTOR

Many who choose the public sector do so because the ideals behind the public services match their own. There are a range of options within the public-sector name tag, however. Possible employers would include NHS trusts, local councils, colleges, and central government departments. The same general rules apply to the public sector as to any other – find out exactly what prospects you are being offered, not only in terms of immediate training and job satisfaction, but looking ahead to promotional opportunities. You should also bear in mind that if you become too closely identified as a purely public-sector accountant you may have trouble transferring into the private sector at a later date, should you want to do so.

As for pay and benefits, public-sector salaries will tend to lag slightly behind their private-sector equivalents, but there are still plenty of well-paid top jobs. The director of finance in a large housing association might get up to the £70,000 mark. A local government finance chief might approach £90,000. There are often compensatory benefits for slightly smaller pay packets which may improve quality of life. Public-sector employees are more likely to receive paternity leave, enjoy generous holiday allowances or find an understanding ear if they want a sabbatical. This isn't to say that public-sector life is a soft option, but some spirit of the greater good apart from just the profit margin does live on.

Competition for public-sector jobs can be tough. The National Audit Office recruits graduates with at least twenty-four UCAS points and a 2.1 honours degree in any subject. The NAO may receive around 800 applications a year for just thirty graduate vacancies. The selection process is very much competence-based, culminating in a selection day during which candidates have to complete a series of around five different exercises. Commitment and teamwork, good communication skills and a capacity for concentrated study are all cited as necessary qualities for applicants. Recent graduate-recruitment programmes have offered a training programme leading to qualification with the ICAEW under its TOPP scheme.

Trainees start their careers as assistant auditors and spend most of their time before qualification working on financial audit assignments, but should also get some exposure to value-for-money audits. Promotion to auditor should follow from completion of the ICAEW's exams, followed by the senior auditor title on qualification. Further up the career chain, management and planning assignments increase.

Working conditions within the NAO reflect its public-sector position, but the organisation is not part of the Civil Service and sets its own pay scales. Though some notice may be taken of the rates paid to Civil Service staff, attention is also given to private-sector scales.

The local government equivalent of the NAO, District Audit, is structured into five regions and employs over 1,000 people, with many working in small, local offices. The agency recruits fifteen to twenty graduates a year to become trainee auditors, receiving anything from 500 to 1,000 applications for those places. New joiners gain twelve months of work experience before beginning to study for the CIPFA qualification. Vacancies spread across England and Wales. Applicants should have a minimum of twenty-two UCAS points and a 2.2 degree. An appreciation of the public services is also preferred, alongside strong numerical and interpersonal skills.

There are also opportunities for people with A levels, or the equivalent, to become trainee audit assistants, although non-graduates do not study for any professional qualifications. Undergraduates can also apply for a twelve-month placement with the agency or the Audit Commission itself. The placement could involve working with auditors in the field, carrying out value-for-money reviews, or supporting managers looking at cost effectiveness and best practice at the Audit Commission's head office in London. District Audit also recruits qualified accountants to work as auditors.

On the public-sector tax side, the Inland Revenue fills most of its jobs in more senior levels by promotion of existing staff, but it does recruit graduates to its own Fast-Stream Development Programme. Competition for Fast-Stream places is tough, with only fifteen to twenty vacancies a year, and applicants need to demonstrate the potential to rise to the Revenue's most senior levels. Most such entrants will spend much of their careers working as senior-level Tax Inspectors, but are likely to spend some time employed in tax policy areas and as managers. In 1997 the Revenue also launched a programme to recruit graduates to train as inspectors, but at that time it was not clear whether this would be repeated. In recent years, most inspectors have been selected from the Revenue's junior ranks and trained up to the role.

Fast-Stream joiners face a demanding training programme including tough exams. Recruits learn about how the tax system works, the economic background and how financial accounts are put together, and taken apart. Training in personal skills such as team working and leadership is also given. Fast-Streamers also consider how to give policy advice to government ministers and look at the strategic management of the Revenue itself. The training is given by a mix of residential courses, tutorials during day visits to regional training centres, self-study and office-based practice. After the first year, most Fast-Streamers go through Core Professional Training which takes eighteen months to complete. Those who enter the Revenue by other routes may take their core training over a period of up to four years. Core Professional Training modules cover specific areas of the direct tax system, including both statute and case law, and tax investigation work.

Apart from these graduate schemes, most applicants to the Revenue enter clerical or junior executive posts and do not require any specified academic qualifications. At non-graduate levels, the Revenue's selection process puts more emphasis on skills than paper qualifications, specifying the areas in which applicants need to demonstrate competence. These include managing people, managing resources, oral expression, written communication, interpersonal skills, analytical skills, decision making and forward thinking. While interpersonal ability and oral expression are considered most important at every level, in junior posts, ability in managing people and resources may be interpreted as essentially effective self-management.

Occasionally the Revenue recruits qualified accountants to work in tax compliance alongside inspectors.

THE APPLICATIONS PROCESS

The accountancy bodies themselves form a key source of information when tracking down that important first job. The ICAEW produces an annual guide to training vacancies, listing the firms in public practice with vacancies that year, both in the UK and overseas. The guide indicates the size of each office, the number of vacancies and the level of entry available, for example graduate only or A level. There is also a much shorter list of commercial and service organisations participating in the TOPP scheme. The 1997 edition listed just five employers with a total of thirty-seven vacancies. The National Audit Office accounted for thirty of these.

In late March or April the ICAI publishes 'Opportunities in Accounting', a list of firms with vacancies coming up for students. It is worth noting that many firms do not put their names forward for inclusion on the list, preferring to confine their recruitment activities to presentations at universities and colleges.

ICAS also produces a *Directory of Training Vacancies*, listing over 400 approved training places with authorised training organisations each year. Most will be in practice, though some are in commerce and industry or the public sector. As a general rule, applications to join accountancy firms can be made at any time of the year. Many joiners start work in the late summer after completing their university finals.

CIPFA publishes a vacancy listing in the autumn on behalf

of employers of CIPFA trainees. The listing details financial-management trainee vacancies with a variety of employers, but only those that CIPFA has been asked to publicise. The October 1996 listing contained jobs with accountancy firms, including five of the Big Six, healthcare trusts and local councils. CIPFA estimates that each year there are around 600 vacancies for CIPFA trainees. Details should also appear in the local press and careers directories.

Prospective management accountants also get help from their potential professional body. CIMA's journal, *Management Accounting*, and the *Directory of Opportunities* it produces will indicate potential employers. Many companies sponsor students through their CIMA training and flag this up in their recruitment advertising. Look for vacancies in the local and national press.

Public-sector jobs will be advertised in the press and vacancy listings circulated around careers offices. The NAO advertises its graduate vacancies through a national advertising campaign at the start of each year. It also attends careers fairs, sends its brochure to careers offices, and advertises in graduate employment directories. District Audit plans to do most of its recruiting between October and Easter and uses mass marketing to attract applicants. For Inland Revenue jobs, the local press or job centres are more likely to be used for junior vacancies, while the national press is used for graduate schemes and more senior vacancies.

Many employers, both professional firms and companies, will use the Milk Round to recruit at least some of their trainee accountants. Employers give presentations and hold first interviews on campus, making an efficient recruitment system for both themselves and their target graduates. The main downside is that your choice of organisation is immediately limited if you use this method of job hunting alone, particularly in terms of smaller companies and firms.

YOUR CV

Once you have found a job to target, you just need to persuade the employer to offer it to you. The first step towards this is to apply in the correct format. Many graduate jobs may call for you to fill in a detailed questionnaire rather than send in a CV. The questionnaire requires much of the same information, such as educational achievements, but will also ask questions targeted to find out how interested you really are in accountancy. One item on the form might ask you to describe occasions where you have shown business flair, for example. Before panicking, think of even the most tenuous example. How about the time you changed the order of your paper round route so you could get the delivery finished faster, making one leg downhill rather than uphill? That shows efficiency and creative thought.

The key to these forms and the CV is to allow plenty of time to get the content and presentation right. Practise filling in a photocopied form so you space your responses correctly. Don't prepare one standard CV and use it for all job applications. Your CV has to be tailored to each job application, emphasising the relevant information that will show you to be a suitable candidate.

The CV needs to:

- confirm that you have the experience, ability and personality needed for the job
- display your achievements in a way that supports your claim to be suited to the job
- explain your career history clearly – unexplained gaps look suspicious
- be short, sharp and specific.

Don't be too long-winded. For a first job you could even use just one page, no more than two. And check your spelling assiduously without just relying on a spell-checking programme. Spell-checkers don't spot when you type 'spill' instead of 'spell'.

INTERVIEW TIPS

People get scared about interviews, but the one thing you really have to do is – prepare. That means thinking hard about the signals you need to give the interviewer to tell him or her you are the right candidate to choose. The interviewer has two key aims: to see whether you appear capable of handling the job, and to decide if you will fit into the organisation. You can use any relevant experience – holiday jobs, even – to show that you have the ability. Beyond that, you shouldn't try to be what you are not, because if your personality doesn't fit the organisation you probably won't be happy there anyway.

Once you know what the employer is looking for, you can tailor your personal sales pitch accordingly. That means doing research about the firm or company and building a thorough understanding of the job for which you are applying. As a general rule, you should try to give the interviewer a positive impression about your achievements to date, your potential, and your enthusiasm. Remember not to get distracted at the interview by thinking about whether you really want the job at all. The point of the interview is to get a job offer. You will have time afterwards to decide whether you really want it.

Take time over your appearance. Accountants work in the business world and need to create a businesslike impression. Research shows that we form an initial judgement about someone in the first few seconds of meeting. The way we dress, act and walk through the door makes the biggest impression, followed by our voice – how we speak, our grammar and overall confidence. It is estimated that what we actually say accounts for less than 10 per cent of the impact we make. What this means for the aspiring accountant is that dressing smartly is essential. Invest in a good suit – it will bring dividends. You don't have to eradicate all signs of your personality, but play the game. Even if you prefer light-coloured suits, research has found that men are considered to carry more authority when wearing dark suits. Polish your shoes. Women should wear tights or stockings and avoid cardigans.

It's not just your clothes that give your character away. Grooming is also vital. Hairstyles should be neat and businesslike. Studies show that women who wear make-up to work are promoted more rapidly. For men, beards often cause a bad impression. You shouldn't feel that you are giving up your individuality by following these norms, but take them seriously. There is nothing worse than turning up to an interview and feeling that you don't look the part. It's bad for your confidence, and bad for your prospects.

The most popular interview questions will cover your reasons behind choosing your school or university courses, and what elements you have found most challenging or satisfying. The interviewer will also try to find out how deeply you have thought about the accountant's life, perhaps asking how you will manage the conflicting demands on your time when training. You may be asked to name your biggest weakness, greatest strength and whether you see yourself as a team player. Have reasons to back up every claim you make. And decide what you will say if asked where you plan to be in five years' time. No one expects you to know for sure, but you need to come up with something positive and realistically ambitious. Never say you hate your current job or course. Negativity is a turn-off. Don't say anything you can't back up. Don't give a precise figure for the salary you are looking for. Don't sound unenthusiastic.

Remember that the interview is a chance for you to find out more about the employer. You might want to ask about the professional and management training provided. What are the opportunities for promotion? What happened to the last person to do your job? If there are many people at that level, ask what the staff turnover is like. What personal attributes does the interviewer consider most important for success in the company? The interviewer will expect you to have questions ready. Don't be caught out.

Ten tips for interview success:

1. Research the employer thoroughly.
2. Think through your answers to likely interview questions.
3. Think of your weaknesses – then think how to put a positive angle on them.
4. Prepare questions to ask the interviewer.
5. Dress in a businesslike manner.

6. Allow plenty of time to travel to the interview. A late appearance will not impress and if you get there early you will have time to have a coffee and compose yourself.
7. Use positive body language – shake hands firmly and maintain eye contact with the interviewer.
8. Answer the questions you are asked and don't waffle.
9. Never imply that accountancy or the employer may not be your first choice.
10. If you get nervous, remember that interviewers get nervous too. If you can both settle comfortably into the interview, you will both gain much more from it.

3
Onwards and Upwards

As a first step on the climb to the top business jobs, accountancy is about as good as you can get. Finance directors in FTSE 100 companies are powerful people in their own right, but if you want to move out of the finance role, there is no reason why you can't. Many chief executives started out in a finance department. Gerry Robinson, chief executive of the Granada group, began his career as a management accountant, gaining the CIMA qualification. David Jones, an ACCA-qualified accountant, moved into the top spot as chief executive of Next plc. ACA Ian Harley took over as chief executive of Abbey National, moving up from his role as finance director.

An accountancy training provides an understanding of the financial building blocks of business. If you want to get to the top, you will need to show you can understand the whole range of business functions, from production to marketing. Personal attributes also become more important the higher up the corporate ladder you climb. An accountancy training gets you started, but a lively mind, leadership, charisma and communication skills will also be needed for the upward path.

THE UPWARD PATH

There are about as many routes to the top as there are leaders in industry. But there are a few rough templates that can be drawn.

The clearest career structure exists in the accountancy firms where there are a number of defined promotional stages.

Taking an audit career as an example, qualification takes around three years, by which time most staff will be titled 'seniors' and be supervising juniors and virtually running small audit assignments by themselves. This stage lasts for a couple of years as wider experience is gained and more responsibility taken for larger audits, special assignments and staff supervision. Seniors who show promise will then be promoted to manager level. The promotion marks a significant shift in the nature of the daily work. The manager acts very much as the co-ordinating linchpin for a large number of jobs. Managers report directly to partners while supervising junior staff who do most of the hands-on work at client offices. The manager will review their documented work, advise on difficult technical issues, monitor client relations, and look for ways to extend the firm's service. If the manager wants to make it to the next level, partnership, evidence will be needed of strong leadership and business skills. That doesn't just mean completing audits on time and within budget, but expanding the services that the firm provides to clients, and thus fees.

The most successful managers may be invited to join the partnership. Given that many staff leave before even getting to senior management level, the proportion of all trainees who make it to partner level is tiny. Becoming a partner may not be attractive to everyone, partly because it generally involves making an investment in the firm. Under this traditional approach, all partners were 'equity partners'. That meant that on becoming a partner they paid in an amount of capital to help fund the business, essentially buying a stake in the firm. Each year they were paid a share of the partnership's profits. When they retired, their investment was repaid.

Now many firms have modified the system, introducing a type of salaried partner, who doesn't buy a stake in the firm. Profit-sharing schemes have also been modified so that the contribution each partner makes, in terms of client and management responsibilities, is recognised in his or her remuneration.

Partners have even more clients assigned to them, but spend far less time on each. They bear the final responsibility for making sure that work has been completed properly and that the client is satisfied. Partners also shoulder the final responsibility for the regulatory aspects of the auditor's job. They will face disciplinary action by their professional body if the firm's standards slip in some way – for example, if a company's accounts are approved only for errors to emerge later and the audit found to have been inadequate. Despite rising up the promotional ladder and supervising the work of others, they still have to keep technically up to date and spend significant amounts of time on the core audit and accountancy work. In some firms, partners will be required to take on additional responsibilities, perhaps the management of staff training and development or marketing. However, the largest firms increasingly use experts in each function, employing trained human resources people and marketing executives, freeing up audit partners to use their expertise to generate fee income.

Partners will choose one of their number to become the senior partner, a kind of chief executive, who heads the firm. Partnerships don't have to disclose the same information about their income and profits as companies do, so no one knows exactly how much most senior partners, or even the average partner, can expect to earn. However, KPMG has incorporated the audit side of its business and gives detailed information about partner earnings in its annual published accounts. Colin Sharman, the firm's UK senior partner, was paid almost £470,000 in the year to 30 September 1996, plus a profit share of £176,000 and pension contributions of £125,000. In other words his total remuneration for the year came to a grand total of around £771,000. Colin Sharman, however, is not typical of the audit profession. KPMG is a giant firm and he sits at the top of it. The largest number of partners received basic remuneration of between £100,000 and £125,000, although they would have received a share of the partnership's profits and pension contributions on top.

Accountancy careers outside the audit firms can be more varied in that the path upwards is less obviously structured. Within a company's finance department there will be a range of promotional levels. The finance director at the top carries responsibility for reporting on the company's performance to shareholders and the other directors on the company's board. Depending on the size of the company, there could be a financial controller and a team of financial accountants helping to pull the company's figures together, as well as controllers responsible for different divisions in the group. You could find management accountants and financial analysts responsible for compiling data which can be used to take management decisions about future corporate policy. For example, if you know which tinned vegetables make the highest contribution to profit in which parts of the country, you can make sure a new store is stocking the right goods. Mushy peas may be more popular in some regions than in others. The day-to-day financial administration will be managed by a team of accounts staff, who will be busy recording the company's financial transactions, running the payroll system, paying suppliers, managing the sales ledger and chasing up late payers.

In all these roles, administrative, analytical, or reporting, the higher you get, the more responsibility you will have for ensuring the company is a smooth-running financial machine.

MOBILITY

In industry, achieving promotion will often require a move to a new company in search of openings at the next level. But mobility is increasing in the accountancy profession in general. In the past it would have been common for an individual to start training with one audit firm and then remain with that same firm, progressing up through the ranks, until retirement. Now it is increasingly common for staff to move between accountancy practices, to gain promotion, to move into a different specialism, or to gain work experience with a different type of client. Again, few people stay with a firm for more than three or four years after qualifying.

Within the large accountancy firms, switching between departments has always been possible, particularly for the best trainees whom the firms want to keep. But increasing competition for staff has made such moves even more widespread.

Within public practice it might be possible to move from audit to tax, insolvency, corporate finance, management consultancy, IT consulting and other specialist departments. The basic rule applies, however – you need to move when still at a junior level. Don't wait too long after qualification, otherwise you may be pigeon-holed in one sector and be considered too senior to start again, learning the ropes in your preferred specialism.

Staff trained in the accountancy firms have a long history of transferring into industry and banking. And some staff, if fewer of them, move from industry and commerce into the audit firms, though most often in a consulting role. Audit and consulting firms trying to strengthen their expertise in a particular industry sector may be interested in recruiting accountants who have trained and worked in that area. For example, CIMA qualifieds leaving industry for practice are less likely to get involved in routine audit work, since they won't have the relevant audit skills. But they might be useful for consulting on special projects, such as the implementation of a new accounting system for a client from their old industry sector.

The increasing fluidity means that accountants do have the ability to shape the direction of their careers, but thinking ahead is important. If you know you want to move into a post with an investment bank in the City of London, then you need to train in an audit division with City and banking clients. You will need to be able to show relevant experience when applying for City jobs.

Movement between public and private sectors has not traditionally been common, but is possible and may increase as private and public sectors interact more closely. For example, government-initiated programmes such as the Private Finance Initiative, where private money is used to help fund public-sector projects, have strengthened the links between public- and private-sector accountants.

CASE STUDY

Jeremy Thomas, aged thirty-three, joined KPMG's Birmingham office as an executive consultant in 1996. He had no idea that he would move into the consulting field when he began his career in industry. After completing a degree in Business Administration at Bath University in 1986, he joined Dowty, the defence group, as a commercial apprentice, essentially a management trainee role.

Dowty sponsored me while I was at university. I worked for the company for eighteen months during my degree course, then for two years after graduating. As a commercial apprentice, you had two possible routes: to move into purchasing or finance. I think they liked us to become accountants and the training course they had was CIMA. I looked into other accountancy qualifications, but CIMA seemed the right choice. I stayed with Dowty until I had passed my final CIMA exams in December 1987. I left because I wanted to get away from engineering and into the fast-moving consumer goods sector, and I also felt I was being underpaid in my current role.

I joined the Hereford cider-maker HP Bulmer and stayed there for the next eight years. I had a range of roles during that time. I was the financial controller of the soft-drinks division, then financial controller of Symonds Cider, a company that Bulmer acquired. I then became a commercial accountant in the cider division at head office. In that role I had to keep financial control of the cider division's revenue and marketing spend and support pricing decisions. I moved on to become operations finance manager with responsibility for all the financial aspects of Bulmer's operations, including manufacturing, distribution, and logistics.

After a while I moved into project work. First, I was seconded to a business strategy review where I spent twelve months working with consultants on restructuring the business. Then I spent another year on a business process re-engineering project, working with yet more external consultants. That experience made me think about consulting as a career option. The work was interesting and the experience of working beside the external consultants made me realise I was capable of doing that type of work myself. But I remained with Bulmer for another year, performing the role of commercial finance manager which was probably the largest role I had at Bulmer. I had responsibility for all the financial aspects of Bulmer's sales and marketing activity in the UK.

Then, in 1996, I took the opportunity to further my career by joining the KPMG consulting practice as a member of the profit-improvement team. Since then, I have worked on a range of projects, including a cost-efficiency review for a utility, a strategy review for a major dairy company and a customer-account profitability study for a shower manufacturer.

I am enjoying the work, which is a good mix of home and away assignments. I have worked away in the north-east for three to four months and I am just starting a job that will involve a month in Southampton. I don't mind working away from home. I like the variety, and it goes with the territory.

One of the great advantages of consultancy is that you can live where you want. I drive for at least an hour, night and morning, to and from clients in the Midlands or the Birmingham office each day. I accept that because I like where I live, but you have to be disciplined. I am on the road by 6.30 a.m.

Consulting is not for people who want to get stuck behind their desks and know what they will be doing next week. If you enjoy a challenge, that's consulting. But if you are status conscious, in the sense of having a number of people working for you in a nice, stable environment and a nice office, then consulting isn't for you. Any status that you have has to be earned. You have to gain respect from each client you deal with.

It's useful to have some experience before moving into consulting. There are people who enter a consultancy at the bottom level and work their way up, right through to partner. I find it a distinct advantage in dealing with clients on consulting assignments to be able to refer back to my time in industry. I feel that I add far more value to them by talking from experience rather than just theoretically. If you have a good few years' experience, it gives you that credibility you need.

SPECIALISATION

The accountancy profession is becoming increasingly specialised. This trend has manifested itself in the accountancy firms in the way that they have reorganised their own structures. The traditional organisation had an audit division, a tax division, and perhaps an insolvency arm. Staff were simply divided along functional lines.

This structure has been revised by many firms. Driven by the need constantly to improve client service and fend off the competition, firms have begun to structure themselves into industry groups. Some audit, tax and consulting staff are brought together to specialise in the retail sector, while another group concentrates on banking, another becomes expert in the utilities, and so on. Where in the past a trainee might work on an insurance company, then a toy manufacturer, then a high-street retailer, now he is more likely to specialise in one type of business.

The advantage for the young accountant is that specialist knowledge tends to be more highly regarded than generalist experience. The young auditor who wants to break into industry will be more attractive to companies in an industry sector where he has gained in-depth knowledge, perhaps of rivals' operations. The disadvantage is that getting stuck in an industry sector you don't like could cramp your ability to move to one you prefer.

Within industry, too, it is easier to move between companies within a particular industry sector than to move into a completely different type of business. And within any particular sector you will need to specialise in a particular type of role – preparing a group's accounts from those of its constituent companies, for example, or taking a strategic financial analyst role.

The increasing degree of specialisation in the accountancy profession can also mean that if you pick a growth area you can improve your chances of rapid promotion. The profession is constantly evolving and developing new areas of work. As the speciality grows, if you get in there early you stand a good chance of rising to the top. The growth sectors may, however, change with time and fluctuations in the economy.

Within the audit and consulting firms there are a number of growth areas that deserve a mention. Forensic accounting has to be one of the sexiest areas of public practice. As the job title suggests, forensic accountants are the people you call on to pick over the evidence when something has gone wrong. That might mean getting to the bottom of a multi-million-pound fraud discovered in a bank's accounts. It could be assessing the true value of an insurance claim for lost profits. Would the business really have generated £50,000 in sales that week if it hadn't had to shut due to a burst pipe? In such a case, the forensic accountant would look at typical trading in other weeks, take account of seasonal fluctuations, and so on. Forensic experts provide reports to help with legal action and may even appear in court as expert witnesses. Their role is that of the financial sleuth. It requires an analytical mind and the discipline and patience to work through piles of potential evidence, be that a list of financial transactions, bank statements, or company accounts, in order to piece together the true accounting story. Forensic accounting has become a boom area since solicitors' rules were changed to allow them to take on cases on a 'no win – no fee' basis. The lawyers need accountants to report on the financial aspects of these cases.

Forensic accountants will often not need to deal with company staff when conducting an investigation. They may simply analyse data handed over by the management, or seized from the business by police. In other circumstances they may be called upon to download computer data at night when no employees are in the office. Sometimes they may be taken into an office in working hours but act as if they are conducting an ordinary business review in order to avoid suspicion. Occasionally they may have to work alongside individuals who stand to lose out from their work, in which case forensic accountants have to show tact mixed with determination.

Another growth area covers the whole range of risk management and regulation. This doesn't just affect accountants in practice. High-profile frauds have forced many companies and banks to tighten up their accounting and business controls in an effort to prevent rogue staff losing them money. For the accountancy firms, there is a growing role for risk-management experts to advise clients on sensible precautions. In the past, such work was associated with internal auditors, who are also enjoying an upsurge in career opportunities. Those working in this area often now describe themselves as working in the more appealingly named areas of information risk management, risk assurance, or business risk consulting. Essentially, this involves looking at a company's systems of controls that are designed to prevent theft, employee error, or any other event that could damage the business performance.

The work focuses heavily on the company's IT systems, making sure they operate correctly and are protected from unauthorised manipulation, but the business risk consultant's remit could range far more widely. More general commercial factors, such as over-dependence on one supplier, could also be considered. What would happen if that supplier went bust? Would the company be able to find a replacement? The work focuses on spotting IT and business weaknesses before they cause problems, and then coming up with solutions.

One of the arts to developing a successful career in accountancy is to spot these trends as they emerge. In some ways this isn't difficult, as the recruitment consultants will be screaming out for candidates to move into growth sectors. However, there should always be opportunities in the specialist sectors such as insolvency, corporate finance, or tax. If you are tempted by one of these options you may need to brace yourself for further exams. In insolvency, for example, many practitioners sit the exams of the Joint Insolvency Examination Board. In fact, you can't be licensed to take on insolvency appointments in your own name without this qualification. Tax specialists may be encouraged to sit the exams set by the Chartered Institute of Tax. If you really can't face the thought of more exam pressure, you should perhaps pick another area.

CASE STUDY

David Logan, aged twenty-eight, is a manager in the business recovery and insolvency (BR&I) department of PricewaterhouseCoopers in Glasgow. A member of the Institute of Chartered Accountants of Scotland, his interest in accounting began when he was still at school.

When I was at school I was always very interested in the numbers side of things and accounting seemed to be a way of using them for a practical purpose. I wasn't interested in the pure academic side. My uncle was an accountant and the things he talked about interested me. I did an accounting degree at the University of Strathclyde and then in 1988 I joined the accountancy firm Deloitte Haskins & Sells, which two years later merged with Coopers & Lybrand, now PwC.

Though the chartered training can be hard, I always enjoyed the variety of work that audit provided and the number of clients you were exposed to. I never liked the exam side of the training, but that was always just a necessary evil. Three weeks after my final exams the partner in charge of the office, who was also in charge of the insolvency department, let it be known he was looking for a recently qualified accountant to join his team. I had an interview and was chosen.

At the beginning of my career I didn't expect to go into insolvency. I had always considered myself to be fairly IT-literate but I found that wasn't where my ability really lay. It became apparent, probably during the second year of my training, that insolvency was the kind of department I wanted to work in. I was interested in that area because corporate recovery and insolvency gives you a more direct involvement in the way businesses operate. This is about looking at what we can do to right historic wrongs. Because of the variety of the work you have to be able to show you can come up with a new solution to a problem because the historic solution may have been found wanting. We do a lot of work on the recovery side, it's not just about closing businesses down. When you work in insolvency, you can have a role a bit like a surgeon, not just an undertaker.

It's also very much a hands-on role. Some people use their training in accountancy as a springboard to go into industry. But when you are appointed to a company as a business recovery and insolvency practitioner your job is much akin to that of a finance director, with sales and marketing thrown in. There is no other profession where somebody at my level would be given that responsibility. And with that responsibility comes experience, and that's what counts.

The work is unpredictable too. Over the years there have been several occasions where I have gone into the office with a basic plan of what I want to achieve that day, and then an assignment comes in. The message comes through, 'Go and get some stuff. You won't be home for a few days.' That's very exciting.

At any point in time, the firm deals with hundreds of insolvency appointments and so the key to the job is to make sure that when something new and unexpected happens, you still have the ability to service existing clients. You need good project-management skills. You can't let one project run away with you.

There are downsides to the job. We do our best to rescue what we can but there are times when companies do cease trading and jobs are lost. That's difficult because although what you are doing may be in the best interests of the clients, it can affect other people's livelihoods.

I plan to stay working in this area. I know it is something I am good at and that I enjoy. I have a side role in forensic accounting too. Both insolvency and forensic accounting involve a similar skill in problem-solving from a particular point of view. You have to look at a company's position and understand what is wrong and what you can do to right those wrongs. You have to have speed of reaction in terms of analysing those problems. You don't have three months in order to bed yourself in at a company. Very often you have a matter of days, if not hours, to find out what the key issues are and how they can be addressed.

The BR&I insolvency business is less cyclical than some people believe. At each point in the economic cycle there are circumstances which lead to companies having insolvency practitioners appointed. A business could get into trouble as a result of poor management.

I think it does make a difference being part of a Big Five firm. The firm has a certain status within the financial market which means it will be considered for confidential appointments. People who appoint us know they will get access to a huge breadth of experience. And bigger firms are not just interested in the bigger appointments. Big firms are interested in any job that allows a rescue to be achieved. The appointment that benefited me most over the years was one of the smaller jobs I have done. I was involved in the rescue of a small village supermarket a few miles outside Glasgow. The shop was a key employer for the village. It wasn't headline-making stuff, but the way we saved the outlet was of great benefit to the community.

CAREER PLANNING AND JOB HUNTING

At some point in your career, you may feel the need for advice on which way to go next. You may be able to discuss your options with your employer. The accountancy firms often appoint a counselling partner with responsibility for steering an individual through the early years. Some use a mentoring system whereby a senior or manager will provide a similar and perhaps more approachable source of support. Your own peer group and those a few years ahead also provide a guide to the areas they consider the most interesting or as providing the best career options.

However, you may feel you need objective guidance from an expert with whom you can talk freely without any danger of your career hopes or doubts being fed back to your employer. Many of the professional bodies provide a career-counselling service for members. The ICAEW, for example, offers recruitment and career counselling through a specialist business arm, Chartac Recruitment Services. Chartac also maintains a page on the ICAEW's web site containing current information on job opportunities and detailing specific job vacancies, which you can find at www.icaew.co.uk/menus/direct/dsab.htm. You can also look out for the personal profiles of leaders in your profession published in your membership body's magazine. These give you an idea of the different routes to the top.

Another option is to visit a specialist recruitment agency. Some may only want to hear from you if you have a particular job application in mind, but others will be prepared to talk through your personal skills and attributes and may come up with a direction you hadn't previously considered. You do need to make sure that you don't get talked into applying for a new job just because it is there. Nor should you accept the first job you are offered, particularly when the economy is doing well and there are many opportunities. Careers advisers say that the experience you get in the early stages of your career after qualification is very important. You need to keep on a healthy learning curve, so choose wisely. For example, newly qualifieds can get tempted into the banking sector by generous salaries, only to find they become stuck in a boring, number-crunching back-room job where they learn little and as a result lose bargaining power when they want to move elsewhere.

If you have a job in mind, you can thumb through the magazines produced by the accountancy bodies. Browsing through the ads will highlight booming areas, locations and the going salary rates. The weekly trade newspaper *Accountancy Age* is also a key source, particularly at junior to mid-management level. The national newspapers should also be scanned for vacancies. Look out for the days when the papers have a regular accountancy or finance slot, such as Thursday in *The Times* and *Financial Times*. These are the days most financial posts will be advertised. Also look out for editions that round up the week's opportunities, such as the *Guardian* on Saturday.

An increasingly popular approach is to look for a job over the Internet. Try the web sites of the types of organisations for which you might want to work. For example, Arthur Andersen's web site at www.arthurandersen.com/firmwide/recruit/index.htm lists openings at its offices round the world. This is a useful exercise not only to see specific vacancies but also to get a feel for the areas in demand both within the UK and internationally. For example, calling up Andersen's Career Opportunities page in the late summer of 1997 highlighted the demand for IT risk consultants to join the firm's Computer Risk Management Division in London, Birmingham, Leeds, Manchester and other major UK cities.

GETTING CREATIVE

There are plenty of opportunities to build variety into an accountancy career. One of the most straightforward ways may be to go to work for a different employer on secondment. Audit firms have a track record of sending staff off to work for external organisations, including clients, banks and government departments.

Before its merger with Price Waterhouse, Coopers & Lybrand required its staff to complete an external secondment in order to be promoted to senior manager. The firm had an extensive secondment programme covering major organisations and government departments, including the Treasury. Though a secondment to a Coopers office overseas would count for the promotion, a stint with a completely different organisation was encouraged. Arthur Andersen is another strong believer in the value of secondments, which the firm sees as important for career development. Though many involve a simple move to a different practice area within the firm or to an overseas office, recent examples have included secondments to clients and financial organisations such as the Bank of England.

Some secondments may involve work of a highly technical

nature. For example, a small number of places are available at the Accounting Standards Board, the body charged with drawing up the UK's accounting rules, called Financial Reporting Standards. The ASB needs a small number of project directors to undertake the job of steering these standards through from concept stage to the issuing of the final public document. These positions require technical ability and interest in the theory behind accounting, one of the more intellectual opportunities among accounting jobs. Traditionally, most of the project directors have been supplied on secondment from the Big Five firms but the ASB welcomes applications from elsewhere too. Those who enjoy the technical side of the accounting profession could also become specialists within an accounting firm, interpreting the work of the ASB for partners and clients. The accountancy institutes themselves have technical departments fulfilling a similar interpretative role for members. There may also be opportunities higher up the career ladder to sit on special committees administered by the ASB to look at issues affecting particular sections of the business community, small-company or public-sector accounts, for example. Technical accounting also reaches beyond the UK's shores. Another body is responsible for issuing international accounting standards which may in time become widely used by UK companies and multinationals around the world.

If you have trained in an audit firm but want a real change, you may be able to arrange a secondment in the charity sector. You may need to do a lot of the organisational legwork yourself, but firms may consider your suggestion if you can present the plan positively. The firm will be more supportive if it sees a benefit to itself, perhaps simply because your own skills will be boosted, or because links with a target sector will grow, or just because you can generate positive publicity. Firms also recognise that secondments can keep staff loyal. Not all employees require pay increases alone as their career develops. Some place a high priority on new experiences and the chance to build up a portfolio of skills. If the firm values you as an employee, it would prefer to loan you on secondment rather than risk losing you for good. Of course, it has to accept the risk that you may not return after the secondment. Don't give them any reason to think you won't.

If you do opt for a secondment, there are three issues you need to clarify before you start. What does your present employer want from your secondment? What does the company where you will spend your secondment want from it? What do you want from it? A secondment shouldn't just be about getting away from one environment because another may seem easier, or more exciting. The firm is sending you in order for you to gain new, or enhance existing, skills. It would also like to think you will build up solid contacts there. The company you go to will be looking to gain from any experience you can bring that differs from that of its own staff. And you should also be looking to pick up new skills. If you haven't got anything new out of the experience that you can use to improve your CV, then the secondment hasn't been a success.

One last creative option concerns the potential to work for yourself. If you train in audit, you could become a so-called sole practitioner, working on your own, preparing the accounts of other self-employed people, advising small businesses or completing other people's tax calculations. You could go into partnership with other accountants. You will need to have some entrepreneurial flair to grow your client base and fee income successfully, but the potential is there. You don't have to stay in practice either. The founders of the Carphone Warehouse were old friends. One, David Ross, went off to get an accountancy qualification, training at Arthur Andersen in London. When the mobile phone retail business took off, a short period after David had qualified, he left the accountancy firm to become Carphone Warehouse's finance director. A successful career also demands that you seize opportunities as they arise.

EQUAL OPPORTUNITIES

The numbers of women entering the profession have grown steadily and although men still make up the majority of qualified accountants, the gap is gradually closing.

Accountancy is often cited as a female-friendly career option: the professional qualification provides evidence of core skills; those skills are highly mobile, with jobs spread across the country, and the potential to work part-time or from home. But all is not perfect. A survey in 1996 by the trade paper *Accountancy Age* and recruitment consultancy Harrison Willis found evidence of persistent sexism. Over half the 1,200 UK qualified accountants surveyed did not believe women and men enjoyed equal opportunities in accountancy. Only around a third thought women had the same chance as men of reaching partnership or finance-director level. Despite this, the conclusion was fairly upbeat. Over 62 per cent thought equality of opportunity would increase over the next five years.

Though men fill most of the top posts in the profession there are examples of high-profile, successful women. The ICAEW has just elected its first woman to become president, Dame Sheila Masters, a partner with KPMG. In industry, high-achieving women finance directors include Rosemary Thorne at J. Sainsbury plc and Kathy O'Donovan at conglomerate BTR.

Accountancy is an attractive career for women for many reasons. It offers the potential to work all round the country and is becoming increasingly flexible, so that negotiating part-time working arrangements may be possible with certain employers. As long as you keep your technical skills up to date it should be possible to take a career break – to raise a young family, for example – and still return to work later. Finally, there is the ultimate option of working for yourself.

None of these options is necessarily easy. As in other professions, women have formed their own support group, Women In Accountancy, run by representatives of the major UK accountancy bodies. The group provides opportunities to share experiences and career information, and runs workshops to give women confidence in their career choices. It publishes supportive material and also aims to provide a single point of contact for employers and public bodies interested in the issues facing women in the workplace. Another group, Workplace 2000, has been set up by the ICAEW to look at wider issues affecting accountants and their working environment. Though largely run by women, the group looks at how long hours, stress and other challenges affect men as well. One of its general goals is to examine ways to shape the working environment into a more supportive one for people of both sexes.

As far as racial equality goes, there is no particular evidence of overt racism amongst accounting professionals. However, there are far more Asian than black accountants working in the UK. An analysis of the ICAEW's entry for 1996/97 showed that 91 per cent were white, 8 per cent Asian and 0.5 per cent black. As with the female intake, there is no reason why those statistics should not improve.

Accountants of any sex and race who network can build up a solid list of contacts. Because the accountancy profession covers such a wide range of activities, in the public and private sector, in industry and practice, there are a large number of specialist groups offering support and networking opportunities. The ICAEW, for example, has audit, tax and corporate finance faculties to represent members working in those fields, run workshops, and hold discussion events. There are other groups for members in business and for people in small firms or working alone. There are also regional societies which arrange social events and talks. All these provide useful opportunities to make contacts within the profession which may be useful not only for the sense of common support they provide but also for developing your career or business. There are assemblies for young accountants such as the Young Chartered Accountants Group, which again offers junior accountants the chance to meet like-minded people from other firms or companies.

CASE STUDY

Catherine Galvin, aged thirty, joined the London office of Price Waterhouse, before its merger with Coopers & Lybrand, after finishing her music degree at Oxford University in 1989. She qualified as a chartered accountant and now works in industry, as a European financial analyst with Motorola.

I chose accountancy originally because I thought that having a professional qualification could be useful for me, as a woman, if I wanted to have a career break. And there are lots of avenues open to you in accountancy. That's a good thing, though now I am not so sure that accountancy is particularly good for women. Working in the profession is probably better than industry, and people are very used to seeing women accountants in junior or middle-management positions. There is no impediment to women at that level. But problems can come higher up. It takes time for attitudes to change.

I didn't think about doing CIMA or one of the other qualifications. I think it is quite easy to move into a commercial role as an ACA, and so you have the option of working in either commerce or practice. I joined a general audit group with PW and during the audit training it was good seeing lots of businesses, but I often felt I wasn't really contributing anything to clients. Instead, I felt I was stopping them getting on with their work.

After I qualified in 1989, I was bored with audit and felt I was on a treadmill so I went into PW's technical department for six months. I fancied going into the office and knowing where I was going to be every morning, and I wanted to strengthen my technical knowledge. I really enjoyed it. I felt I was learning something and that I could offer something useful.

But I definitely didn't want to continue auditing so I decided to move into industry. I got a job with Unilever doing group consolidation work, more because it was a good company name to have on my CV rather than because I thought it was a particularly good job in terms of experience. The role firmed up my technical skills but it wasn't commercial. I was very much a number cruncher. I stayed for two years and then began to look for another move.

In 1995 I joined Motorola where I was brought in to review the group transfer pricing methodology, making it more efficient and tax compliant. At that time I had no tax experience and so I knew I would learn a lot. After a year I took over the foreign-exchange role too. I look at our foreign-exchange exposures and tell our head office treasury department what forward contracts to take out each month. At first I thought that would involve more of a treasury role, but it is really about understanding the business.

In terms of job satisfaction, I like doing anything that can make the business operate more efficiently – for example, if I can see a computer programme we can use to cut out unnecessary work so people don't spend their time crunching numbers but can think about what they are doing.

My advice to people starting out is to think carefully about your first job. If you qualify with a blue-chip company or Big-Five accountancy firm, that has an unfair effect on the rest of your career. The first job move you make after qualifying is also very important. You need to think about the experience you will get. I think I almost made a mistake. Unilever was a very good name to have on my CV, but I think I could have moved straight into a role like the one I have now, which would have been better for me.

THE REWARDS

In accountancy, as with many other professional sectors today, the question to ask is not 'How much will I earn?' but 'How much do I want to earn?' Pay and benefits vary hugely depending on a wide range of factors, so if earning top pay is important to you, think ahead when picking your sector. For example, in general, public-sector pay lags behind the private sector. Having said that, any accountants who get near the top of their particular sector will never have to worry too much about their bank balances. As young accountants rise through the ranks, the traditional perks of the business world begin to appear, such as the company car, the pension scheme and share options.

Key salary factors include:

- *Size of organisation.* A multinational will pay more than a small domestic company. Managers in the Big Six will take home more than peers in a small firm.

- *City versus industry.* The City wins. Big bucks are still more generally found in the banks of the City of London than in UK Business Ltd.

- *Private sector versus public.* Most people working in the public sector do so because it fits in with their value system. Pay will almost always be lower than elsewhere.

- *London against the regions*. Salaries in London should be slightly higher, but then so is the cost of living.

- *Rare expertise*. Specialists in an expanding sector can command higher rates.

Salaries tend to rise fast when the economy is healthy, but as a rough guide, recruiters Robert Half International published a salary survey in spring 1997. In industry, newly qualified chartered accountants in Greater London could earn £28–35,000, while CIMA newly qualifieds earned just slightly less and ACCAs attracted £24–30,000. Higher up the promotional scale, the type of qualification matters less. Heads of financial or management accounts could expect to earn £35–45,000 in a large company, while financial controllers commanded £45,000 plus. Finance directors in large businesses started on £70,000. Tax and treasury specialists lay in a broad band from £45–80,000, while internal auditors had a range of £45–70,000. Outside London, salaries vary hugely. An internal auditor in a large company in the north might earn £33–43,000. Credit controllers in large, Greater London companies could be paid £17–25,000, while ledger clerks fell in a scale from £17–19,000.

In City and banking jobs, the pay is generally higher than in industry, while in the public sector the remuneration, in financial terms at least, is somewhat less.

Within accountancy practices, newly qualified ACAs in Greater London earned £25–35,000 while ACCA qualifieds received £20–25,000. Assistant managers of any qualification brought home £28–35,000, managers £33–45,000 and senior managers £45–60,000. Partners would be on £80,000 upwards. Tax and insolvency specialists would receive slightly more.

THE FRUSTRATIONS

Many of the worst frustrations occur early on in an accountancy career. Acquiring the technical knowledge and passing exams can seem like a long, hard struggle. Higher up the promotional chain, job satisfaction should improve as increased experience brings greater decision-making authority.

There will always be some frustrations, however. Auditors complain often about the increasingly litigious environment and the traditional lack of any limits on the liability that auditors face in a legal battle. That could mean that a firm could lose a high-profile legal case and go bust, wiping out the partners' personal assets in the process. So far, this has never happened, but unless the law is changed to limit auditors' liability, it could. Otherwise the general downsides to any business life apply. To be successful you may have to put in long hours of hard work in the office with the usual resulting risks to health and family life. But that's an optional price and not all sectors or all employers demand it.

CASE STUDY

Norman Murray, aged forty-nine, is head of Deutsche Morgan Grenfell's private equity business and chief executive of Morgan Grenfell Development Capital (MGDC). He is now chairman of the British Venture Capital Association which represents all those involved in the business of raising funds for new and growing companies. A council member of the Institute of Chartered Accountants of Scotland, he has been involved in venture capital, banking and corporate finance work for seventeen years. But on leaving Heriot-Watt University, training to be an accountant was the last thing he wanted to do.

I did an accountancy course at university as part of my degree. I hated it. I recently found my notes and on the last day of the last lecture of the last year I wrote, 'Thank God, no more of this.' But I then went to work as a graduate trainee for Scottish & Newcastle Breweries and I spent a lot of time working for the finance director. He told me I should think about doing accountancy as it would enhance my career opportunities, and I did.

I joined the firm of Arthur Young McLelland Moores in Edinburgh, who were Scottish & Newcastle's auditors. I didn't particularly enjoy the training but I got through and qualified in 1976. I realised later that the training I had was very good when I went to Hong Kong with another firm, Peat Marwick Mitchell, which was a terrific experience. They did a whole host of large audits and small local textile and trading companies.

After three years I came back to the UK and a job came up with the Royal Bank of Scotland in the corporate finance department. At that time I felt I had learnt enough in the profession and I wanted to do something else, so I took the job in corporate finance which involved advising and providing finance for private companies in the form of both equity and debt. When the bank bought Charterhouse I became a director of Charterhouse Development Capital which is the oldest and most established private equity company in the UK. In 1987 I completed the Executive Education Programme at the Harvard Business School. One of the qualifications required for joining the programme was that you had worked for some fifteen years, so that meant everyone had been doing real jobs. There were people from around twenty different countries, from engineers to accountants to lawyers to bankers, so you got a good mix of views.

Then in 1989 I was head-hunted to join MGDC on its establishment. MGDC now has funds under management for private and unquoted companies of US$1 billion with operations in Edinburgh, London, Paris, Milan, Hong Kong and Singapore. We raise money for a management buy-out fund by presenting to potential investors around the world who will hopefully contribute to the fund. Then we invest in companies that need finance for an MBO or for further development and sit on their boards of directors until it is time to sell our stake. Investments can range from an engineering company to an advertising company and I have sat on the board of a helicopter company, the British School of Motoring, a whisky company – the variety is tremendous.

I don't have a typical day – my work is so varied. It's irregular and unscheduled work. I will visit the US, Middle East and Japan over the next six months. I should have been in South Africa this week, but then something else came up in connection with an investment we were about to make and in the end we completed that deal at 3.30 a.m. on Saturday morning. One of the good things about the job is the excitement of doing deals. That deal could have gone away, it could have fallen through. You have to have an appreciation of negotiation. You negotiate yourself into a better position.

The downsides of the job are also due to the variety. You get calls at all times and if someone calls you up, he wants to feel he is the most important person calling you that day. You also have to prioritise your time, which can be difficult. It's not a nine-to-five job. I had made arrangements to take my wife out on Friday night, but when that deal came up, my family plans were scrapped.

It wasn't automatic for me to go into accountancy, but now I think it's the best thing I ever did. I am now a council member of the Institute of Chartered Accountants of Scotland and I would advise everyone to do accountancy. Going on into corporate finance or venture capital is a good use of the qualification. You need to have good commercial sense, good financial sense and a distinctive personality. But if you have those, the prospects are very good.

Snakes and Ladders

It would be a bold claim for any profession to state that its members will always be in demand. Accountants in all their forms are certainly not insulated from the trends that continue to shape the modern working environment, be they economic or sociological. During the recession some audit firms laid off junior staff because there simply wasn't enough work to go round. Ten years ago, computer skills were an optional extra for senior levels. Now they are an essential. Accountants have to keep up to date, not only in their specialist accounting and tax knowledge, but also with new technology.

THE CHANGING ENVIRONMENT

It's a fairly safe bet that the world as we know it will always need accountants. What is less straightforward is predicting exactly what those accountants may be doing, and who will be employing them to do it.

All sectors of the accountancy profession have heard the hand of progress knocking on the door. Auditors, both in the largest and smallest firms, have had to adapt to a variety of factors, cost pressure being just one. During the last recession, companies began making increasing demands on their auditors and other advisers to cut their fees to a minimum. By law, companies above a legally defined threshold have to appoint a firm of auditors to review their annual accounts, but there is no law that requires them to pay generously for it. A number of financial scandals and high-profile corporate crashes also tarnished the image of the auditor, who became increasingly seen as a necessary evil, an expensive nuisance. Companies began playing one audit firm off against another, inciting a fee-cutting war that led to accusations that audit firms were offering extremely cut-price audits in an attempt to win other, more lucrative, consulting work.

Within the accountancy firms themselves, staff came under increasing pressure to complete audit assignments faster and more efficiently than ever before. The spread of computer-assisted audits helped cut costs as firms devised new methods of working, reducing the manual labour involved.

Fee pressure tends to vary with the state of the economy, limiting the amount firms can do to protect their income. However the recessionary belt-tightening forced them not only to streamline the audit process, but also to explore new ways to sell other 'value-added' services to clients. Such services have more in common with consultancy work – for example, profitability reviews that could consider more efficient ways to finance debts, improve stock control, or control revenue growth. Partners at the top of firms are measured on the new income they bring in, as well as the quality of their audits. The ability to spot new product opportunities and sell them to clients has become another skill required of the high-flying auditor.

With increased cost pressure and increasingly demanding clients, there has been considerable speculation about the future for middle-sized firms. Doommongers have predicted that many will be forced to merge with larger firms, or join forces with each other. Nevertheless, these firms continue to talk positively about the career prospects they offer and some have devised a strategy to become specialists in particular fields, as a way to forge a profitable future.

Question marks were raised about the viability of the smallest accountancy firms after the audit requirement was abandoned for small companies. Here, too, accountants had to come up with a convincing argument for clients to persuade them their services were still useful. In some ways, the change has focused attention on the business advisory side of the general practitioner's role, which everyone agrees is the more interesting part of the job.

Auditors have also been campaigning for some time to have the law of joint and several liability changed. What this law means is that an equity partner in an audit firm can be sued for all his or her personal assets alongside other partners, or instead of them. Imagine you are a partner in the Birmingham office of a Big-Five firm and a partner you have never met in London makes a dreadful error in the handling of an audit. The client goes bankrupt and creditors and investors sue your firm. You had nothing to do with that client, yet if the firm loses the court case, the damages will be so great that you risk losing your home. The audit profession doesn't think this is fair and has been campaigning for the Government to bring in limited liability so that personal assets would be protected. Change seems probable at any time.

Government-led changes are an unpredictable influence on the accountant's life. In 1996 the Inland Revenue introduced a new system for calculating and collecting tax. This new self-assessment system put more emphasis on taxpayers calculating their own tax bills and sending off cheques for the right amount. Theoretically, this could boost the work of small firms of accountants and tax advisers, but it has also triggered interest from other types of mass-market financial service companies. UK banks began offering a tax administration service, and a US company also entered the market offering very basic help but for a cheap price.

In other sectors, too, the pressure has been on to step up efficiency. In the public sector, the National Health Service came under increasing scrutiny from the Conservative Government. Increasing numbers of managers were brought in with a brief to improve efficiency and the role of the accountant rose in importance. But there now seems to be a swing in sympathy away from the administrators towards the health carers, bringing added pressure for financial staff. In banking, the prospects for accounting staff are closely linked to the state of the economy. Accountants in industry are affected in the same way as any other worker. If there is one type of accountant who enjoys a business boom when times are hard, it is the insolvency expert. That means, however, that when the economic good times return, insolvency specialists have to concentrate on selling their corporate restructuring skills, helping struggling companies do better, since fewer actually go bust.

STAYING FRESH

You could say accountants are lucky. The majority are forced to keep their skills sharp by the regulations set by their professional institutes. Most of the professional bodies require their members, even after passing their exams and fulfilling work-experience requirements, to keep up to date. That may mean completing so many hours of training courses each year and reading technical literature on tax and accounting issues. To a certain extent, accountants have to keep up to date – if they don't, they won't be able to do their job anyway. You won't get very far as a tax adviser if you don't follow the tax changes in the Budget or as an auditor if you don't stay aware of new legal requirements for companies filing their annual accounts. Accountants in industry face less regulation, but again market forces will keep them attentive to change. Those in financial-reporting roles need to follow changes in accounting rules, for example.

Given the increasing competitiveness of working life in practice, industry and commerce, accountants who want to rise to the top need to develop a broad range of skills, not least the 'touchy–feely' interpersonal skills. The higher you get up the seniority ladder, the more you will have to demonstrate that you can lead your staff, inspire clients or business partners, and exercise judgement under pressure. If you can't, it will be far harder to make it to the next promotional rung.

The best employers, whether in public practice or industry and commerce, will see an investment in staff training as a benefit to the business as well as to the individuals concerned. The giant audit firms have huge training budgets, as do commercial multinational organisations, and many will conduct their own in-house courses. The professional bodies themselves often run courses, for a fee, but there are increasing numbers of private conference and training companies offering similar services.

TEMPORARY CAREER OPTIONS

Anyone looking for a high degree of variety in their working life can benefit from the temping opportunities an accountancy qualification provides. Temping can also be of use to people unsure of their long-term career direction and wanting to sample different types of companies. Anyone suddenly made unemployed can also be fairly sure of generating income by taking short-term assignments. A large number of agencies are constantly on the look-out for part- and fully-qualified individuals to add to their books.

Companies, accountancy firms and public-sector bodies all make use of temporary staff. This is partly a reflection of the general trend in working patterns away from permanent, lifelong job contracts towards more flexible contracts between employer and employee. It also simply results from the fact that many organisations find their need for financial staff fluctuating over the year. The heaviest workload comes when preparing the annual report and accounts and extra help may only be needed at that time. Special projects, such as a merger with another company or the implementation of a new accounting system, may cause a sudden, temporary increase in the workload which the existing finance team cannot absorb. At such times, the logical business answer is to call a temping agency.

UK accountants don't have the temp market to themselves, however. Many young accountants from Australia and New Zealand come to the UK, particularly London, after qualification and take temporary posts. Some employers even prefer to use Antipodeans, many of whom are prepared to work long hours in order to earn enough money to travel round Europe and the rest of the world.

INTERIM MANAGEMENT

Similar to temping in concept, interim management recognises that companies' demand for particular skills varies. The difference is that interim management implies the use of professionals at a higher seniority level than the standard temp. Interim management is also less likely to be a response to seasonal fluctuations in workload. Interim managers are more likely to be called in to provide specific expertise for a particular project – say, restructuring a division, handling the merger of two businesses, selling off an operating group.

Interim managers have the chance to work with a wide variety of organisations and are well rewarded, both financially and in terms of job satisfaction. The role is also popular with people who want to make a life-style choice about their career. For example, interim managers could, if they chose, take a long break each year, since they don't have to account for their actions to any employer.

Not surprisingly, interim managers need to have gained a high degree of experience before they can enter such a field. They are usually expected to come in to a client and 'hit the ground running'. This type of work requires considerable confidence and charisma, good interpersonal skills and flexibility. Interim managers are perhaps most similar to management consultants, the main difference being that the interim manager has a more hands-on position, with direct responsibility for implementing solutions to problems as well as defining the problem in the first place.

TRANSFERABILITY OF SKILLS

Accountancy offers many different paths in many sectors of society – private companies, public bodies, charities and banks. Despite that range, you may find that, having qualified, there is nothing that seems quite right for you in the traditional accountancy career path. This is where an accountancy training can score again in the flexibility stakes because it can be used as a key to a range of very different jobs. Some trained accountants use their knowledge directly, while others simply build upon it.

LECTURING IN ACCOUNTANCY COLLEGES

Newly qualifieds who want to try something different but make the most of their hard-won technical knowledge could consider a move into accountancy tutoring. The demand for accountants has spawned a whole industry of specialist colleges focused on teaching trainees the accounting knowledge they need to get through their professional exams. The tutors are themselves qualified accountants and most move into the field soon after passing their own exams. They are technically right up to date and are generally expected to have passed all their exams at the first attempt.

Teaching in these colleges could provide a lifelong career. The colleges extend all round the UK and since the demand for accountants shows little sign of slowing, this should also be a fairly dependable career. Unless you move into a managerial role, you have to be prepared to put up with the inevitable repetition involved in teaching the same subjects over and over again. But you might get involved in developing the training company's business, setting up schools in other parts of the country, tendering for new contracts with accountancy employers and recruiting new staff.

To be a successful tutor, you need to be good at explaining potentially complex accounting concepts in a simple way. Patience is vital, as is the ability to encourage students who may take longer to pick up new ideas than the brightest sparks in the class. Tutors may also be expected to provide counselling to students who seem to be struggling, get tough with those who fail to do the necessary studying, and write reports on the progress of students for the firms and companies employing them.

Anyone truly inspired by the subject matter of accountancy with a desire to conduct research could go one step further and become a university lecturer. You will probably need a Ph.D. and will definitely have to be prepared to take a pay cut. Tutors in training colleges teaching accountants in business or practice earn business-related salaries. Academics do not.

PUBLIC RELATIONS

An accountancy training gives you an insider's understanding of the world of finance and the particular sector in which you train. Even if you decide you don't want to remain an accountant, you can use that insider's insight to head off in another career direction. You don't have to throw away all that financial and accounting knowledge, which will be attractive to employers in other lines of business.

Accountants with good communication skills, both written and oral, can move into financial public relations (PR). All the big accountancy firms have PR professionals or press officers, either on their own staff or contracted through an agency. If you have trained with a large accountancy firm or company, you may be able to make a direct internal move from the accounting front line to the PR desk. If there are no openings in your firm, another may be keen. The agencies themselves are eager to hear from people with a financial background, as long as they have the right personality. Press and public relations people need to be outgoing, confident, and personable. They may also have to be prepared to work long hours, even if that work means hosting a cocktail party for the organisation's business contacts.

RECRUITMENT CONSULTANCY

Recruitment consultancies who specialise in supplying permanent and temporary staff to business and finance clients will also be interested in someone with an accountancy background who knows early on that they want to make a career change.

The advantage to the consultancy is that, coming from the accountancy world, you will have a personal understanding of the kind of person who will fit into particular working environments. You will be able to talk to applicants with a confidence based on a common grounding in finance. This won't be enough to get you the job, however. Recruitment consultants need strong personalities to drum up business and develop solid relations with client companies. Communication skills and persistence will be needed. You also need to be a sharp judge of character, knowing how to get behind an interviewee's projected image to find out his or her true strengths and weaknesses.

This is also a sector where job opportunities bear a direct

relation to the strength of the economy. When the economy is thriving and business confidence is up, companies are more likely to be looking for staff and employees are more confident about changing employers. The recruiter will be busy. When times are hard, job vacancies fall and the recruiting business is directly hit. In the last recession, recruitment consultants were among the casualties and those that kept their jobs worked long hours.

WILD CARDS

The key point to remember when looking for a new angle on your accountancy qualification is that your knowledge is useful to people in related fields, even publishers and journalists. So go for something completely different. You could try writing about accountancy and finance. Trade and professional magazines may be interested in taking on people with a financial background even if they have no experience in journalism. The paper trades financial expertise for training in the craft of writing good copy. It's by no means a common option, but an example of the way that starting out through one door, such as accountancy, can lead you into a completely different area from the one you expected.

CASE STUDY

Rita Purewal, aged thirty-one, swapped accountancy qualifications when her first experiences in auditing didn't meet her expectations. Now company accountant with Wolverhampton Wanderers FC Ltd, she has no regrets.

I graduated in Accountancy and Finance from Liverpool University in 1987. I joined a chartered accountancy firm and started auditing, but it was so rigid I felt I couldn't show my potential. It wasn't good for someone like me who is quite creative. I had a view of what accountancy should be, but my first experiences at work didn't live up to that. I was quite disheartened and nearly decided not to carry on. I felt comfortable with figures and felt there was more to accountancy than number crunching.

I stayed with the firm for eight months, but I knew audit was not for me. I looked at the ACCA qualification and saw how flexible it was. It was so diverse in its subject matter. You could work in industry, commerce, private practice, any sort of field. So I switched from the ICAEW to the ACCA and joined a major leasing company in Windsor as assistant accountant, studying in the evenings. I stayed there two years and enjoyed the position.

After getting married, I moved to Birmingham and got a job straight away with Friendly Hotels plc, a £30 million turnover company, as an assistant accountant. In the space of about six to seven months I made quite a lot of improvements in the reporting system and consequently got promoted to management accountant. It gave me such a sense of satisfaction, speaking to the hotel managers, introducing them to the budgeting process via PCs. After two years I was promoted to deputy group financial controller. While working at Friendly Hotels I got my ACCA qualification and, about two weeks later, became pregnant. I didn't really stop working during my pregnancy, but worked at home on my PC as I didn't want to lose touch with what was happening.

I returned to the office four months after my son was born. I got a lot of family support, so I was able to do that. At this point I decided it was time for a career move. I got a letter from a recruitment agency about a job at Wolverhampton Wanderers Football Club, went to the interview and was amazed. The club has one of the best stadiums in the country and I was surprised how multifaceted its business was. Over half the turnover comes from commercial activities. We have a health and fitness club, bars, conference and banqueting facilities, an Internet service, etc. I was not particularly interested in football but I felt that initially this helped me in my vision because I was not blinkered by a passion for football and so could view the club as a commercial business entity.

Since I joined the club in 1994, my whole outlook and perception of football has completely changed. I am passionate about the club and live and breathe Wolves. It's very difficult to work for a club like this and not feel passionate about it. This has also been the turning-point in my career. When I joined Wolves, they didn't have a company accountant – it was a new position. The accounting systems were very limited. The company secretary did the accounts as part of his job, using a manual-ledger system. I was brought in to computerise the accounting system and create a finance function. I set about computerising the accounting process, but six weeks after I came in, the company secretary resigned.

So for the next three months I also performed the company secretary's role which was one of the most exciting times in my career so far. I was suddenly thrown into the world of football and experienced at first hand the hectic and exciting dealings of a First-Division club in the height of the busy season. I handled transfer deals and had the valuable experience of working with Graham Taylor.

I learnt so much in those three months about football itself, but I felt I had so much more to offer on the accountancy side and saw how the business could be developed further. So I moved back to my original accounting role and since then have gone from strength to strength. I installed a fully computerised accounting system and restructured the whole of the company's financial-reporting system. We have created a strong accounts department with a hard-working, dedicated and professional team of five. My specific responsibilities include overseeing the whole of the accounting function whilst continually improving financial controls and developing further the financial information content. The managers are now accountable for their activity centres and controls have been introduced. Before, a department could not assess how profitable it was.

This has been a fantastic experience. I feel very privileged, because not everyone gets the chance I have had. You have to seize any opportunities when they arise and make the most of them. There are still many more challenges for me at Wolves as we are still expanding our operations. I feel I am quite young to be in the position I am and it would be an ambition to achieve a directorship position here. Also I have had that experience of reporting to the Board for two to three years now. I feel quite fortunate about this, because most people don't get that experience at company-accountant level. However, at the back of my mind I know life doesn't begin and end at Wolves and there are plenty of opportunities out there.

Quite a few people write to me, especially Asian girls, as I am seen as a role model. Being a woman and being ethnic, you do have to try that little bit harder, but a lot depends on the culture of the company that you are working within. We are lucky at Wolves as we have a young, progressive management team. It is important to stress that for those who have the ambition and determination, there are so many opportunities out there in the accountancy field. There is no reason why you can't balance being a mother with having a career, providing you have a good support unit. I used to work very long hours at the beginning. Now we have more staff and I can delegate more. I make a point of not working at weekends so I can spend time with my son.

With accountancy, you have got to see it through for the first couple of years and not be disheartened, because it's so important to get a qualification under your belt. I think it is invaluable to be able to work and study at the same time, although it is hard. If you get through the early years and you achieve your qualification, you are then in a much stronger position to be more selective about your career path. It's a very fulfilling and rewarding career and a great basis for so many other things. I enjoy working with people and have enjoyed doing training courses and public speaking. Consultancy work is another avenue I may want to pursue in the future, but most of all I enjoy helping people to achieve their goals and ambitions.

5 Opportunities Abroad

One of the beauties of an accounting career is that money, and what you do with it, is a world-wide concern. Even better, UK-trained accountants are held in high esteem, so there are plenty of opportunities to spend time working in another country.

If you are flexible about exactly where you work, your chances of foreign travel are greatly enhanced. There is fierce competition to get to the most popular destinations, such as Australia and the USA. However, there are many opportunities to work in Eastern Europe as local businesses become increasingly westernised in their approach and multinational companies and firms seek to establish a firm footing and cash in on the growth of these emerging economies. Whether you train in practice, industry or the public sector, there are a range of foreign options open.

ACCOUNTANTS IN PRACTICE

Auditing and financial consultancy is big business. It's also international business. The largest firms, particularly the Big Five and some of those in the following group, send hundreds of staff abroad every year. Trips can be short – for example, helping with the audit of a foreign subsidiary. Or they could involve a secondment to a sister firm overseas and last a couple of years.

The hottest competition for secondments abroad comes just after qualification. Flushed with exam success, many young accountants feel in the mood for adventure and new experiences, particularly if they haven't any family commitments. After years of studying, many newly qualifieds are tempted by the thought of flying off to the sunshine in Sydney and being able to enjoy weekends on Australian beaches.

Many firms offer secondments through a system of swapping staff between offices. So if you go to Paris for two years, a Parisian will take your place in London. These secondments aren't automatic. They take considerable organisation and negotiation between the offices involved. They are sometimes seen as a way of rewarding the best staff and keeping them motivated to stay with the firm. What all this means is that during recessionary times the firm may be less concerned about staff retention, since its own work may be slackening off, and less willing to put in the effort to make a transfer happen. During the last UK recession there was a distinct tail-off in the numbers of newly qualified staff packing their bags for another continent. Only the very best stood a chance. But as businesses picked up world-wide, since the early 1990s prospects have improved.

Competition for destinations such as Sydney and New York is fierce. Secondments there carry prestige and bring the added benefit that there are no language difficulties to worry about. If you think you may want to try to go to a popular foreign destination, make sure you work hard during your training contract. Get noticed as an achiever, and then discuss your interest in going abroad early on, even before you qualify.

For the less choosy, there is a wide range of locations to consider. Each year PricewaterhouseCoopers sends staff to around sixty different countries, covering Europe and China, North and South America, the Caribbean, Africa and the Middle East.

With European moves, it isn't always necessary to be fluent in the local language. Those who can only order a couple of beers in French or Italian may still be able to get to Paris or Milan. Firms will pay for language training if they have enough confidence that the individual will be able to cope. If you are already fluent, so much the better: your chances of getting the plane ticket are far greater. A move within continental Europe does have the advantage of avoiding problems over work permits. Many governments outside the EC may only grant permits where it can be shown there are no locally trained candidates available to fill the post. The US and Canada can be particularly tricky on this point. It is not unknown for accountants to be celebrating the receipt of a job offer in Canada only to be refused a work permit. You are more likely to avoid the problem by getting an internal transfer to an overseas office organised by your existing employer.

One other word of warning. The best opportunities for overseas transfers lie in audit. Tax skills are harder to transfer to a foreign office since so much of the work depends on local law. You can still get employment abroad, but it will be harder to find. So if you are sure you will want to go abroad at some point, stick to the audit and accounting side of the profession.

INDUSTRY AND COMMERCE

Multinational companies also have openings overseas for staff with the urge to roam. Young accountants who trained in a commercial role and those moving out from an audit firm are both sought after.

Where the best opportunities lie at any one time will be affected by the relative booms around the world. For example, as Frankfurt expanded into a key European financial centre in the 1980s, so demand for UK-qualified accountants there soared. Merchant banks were crying out for German-speaking accountants, particularly those with experience of auditing banking clients.

The opening up of business within Eastern Europe has also created many challenging opportunities for young accountants who are not put off by the thought of working in a financial environment less well developed than the UK's. Much of the work is project-oriented – for example setting up internal control and reporting systems and then training local staff to take them over and run them efficiently. An understanding of business life in these countries may be valued by employers once you come back to the UK, but they aren't the easiest locations to visit. Moscow became notorious among recruiters, who had to warn job candidates about the rabies and diphtheria outbreaks, not to mention the corruption associated with some businesses there.

As with accountants in practice, North America is a tougher target. Your best chance of getting there is by joining the UK subsidiary of a US multinational and networking hard. Find a role that requires you to liaise with your American counterparts and will give you a chance to build up contacts in the USA. Make a point of being friendly and helpful when any US colleagues visit the UK and let management know of your wish to work in the States. It may be possible to engineer a rotation across the Atlantic in a couple of years, perhaps swapping with an American employee who wants the experience of working in the UK.

One of the best options in industry for those seeking foreign travel is to take an internal audit position in a multinational. This is a growth area for accountants as companies realise the importance of establishing strong systems and controls, not only as a means of minimising the risk of fraud, but also to make the business run as efficiently as possible. As a result, there are many openings in internal audit. If you work in a company with many overseas operations as an internal auditor you could find yourself flitting round the globe from one group company to the next on a series of short stays. Some internal auditors spend 85 per cent of their time abroad.

You have to be prepared for the particular stresses that come with this kind of travel. There is never enough time to put down roots or make close friends at the companies you visit. International hotels tend to be pretty much alike and constant air travel can be tedious. Keeping up the enthusiasm to spend three weeks at a time in Frankfurt becomes harder once family commitments and children enter the equation. However, for the newly qualified and single accountant, the job offers a variety of foreign experience that's hard to beat. Internal auditors have the chance to visit many more destinations than would be possible on a simple overseas transfer. They also build up an excellent understanding of the different operations within a multinational business, something that they can use to sell themselves when applying for promotions later.

PUBLIC SECTOR

In general terms, there are far fewer opportunities for accountants trained in the public sector. This is simply due to the nature of most public-sector organisations, which are UK based, and the fact that accountants who qualified with CIPFA are not generally recruited by professional practices or by multinational companies for overseas positions, if at all. However, the National Audit Office does send some staff abroad, though generally on very short-term assignments of perhaps just a week. These generally centre around the audit of government agencies and departments abroad, such as Foreign Office embassies and consulates. There may be the chance for longer-term secondments with United Nations or European organisations, though these are even less common.

VOLUNTARY SERVICE OVERSEAS

CIPFA qualifieds, along with other qualified accountants, stand a good chance of overseas work experience if they are prepared to gain it through a placement by Voluntary Service Overseas (VSO). Developing countries don't just value the skills of health workers or irrigation experts. Financial professionals have a lot to offer – for example, training local staff to manage the accounts of a local organisation, or advising on financial control systems. In recent years, VSO has sent individual accountants to work as an accounts trainer in Vanuatu, a senior accountant in the Solomon Islands, a district accountant in Zambia, an accounts lecturer in the Pacific and a government accountant in Bhutan.

Volunteers should have at least two years' work experience after qualifying as an accountant with one of the established accountancy bodies, including the chartered accountancy institutes, the ACCA, CIPFA, CIMA and AAT. But it takes more than professional and technical ability to be accepted by

VSO. Candidates' personalities are vitally important and they will be tested by a series of individual and group activities during the selection process. Volunteers may find themselves working in isolated communities and certainly in a culture very different from their own and so strength of personality is essential. They also have to be adaptable and show respect for other cultures.

This isn't an option for anyone putting financial rewards as a high priority. Pay is at local rates and volunteers are not expected to save any money during the two years that most placings last. Those unable to commit a full two years to VSO may be able to get a short-term placement (STP). Although there are few STPs, the number is increasing and some are available in business and professional positions.

For those with the stamina and self-reliance, the experience can be a rewarding one. Huw Morgan gave up his job as an audit manager to work with the Maldives Monetary Authority which acts as a banker to the Maldives government. Huw was the only qualified accountant working there and his role involved developing appropriate accounting systems while training local staff to manage these systems.

Stephen Masson, another qualified chartered accountant, spent two years working as a finance management adviser for the Lutheran Aid to Medicine in Bangladesh (LAMB) Hospital in Parbatipur. The hospital had fifty in-patient beds and also handled around 300 out-patients a day. Stephen's job included normal day-to-day financial management, budget preparation, and the completion of funding proposals and financial reports for appropriate agencies. Training local staff was again a high priority, including the training of his own successor. Once back in the UK, Stephen returned to the audit profession as an audit manager responsible mainly for charities.

FINDING THAT OVERSEAS POSITION

The same basic rules apply to the job hunter looking to go abroad as to the accountant switching jobs within the UK. Successful hunters are specific about what they want and realistic about the suitability of their experience for their preferred role.

Those who know from the beginning that foreign travel will be important to them should bear that in mind right at the start of their careers when applying for their training contract. If you want to train with an accountancy firm, your best bet will be to pick a Big Five office that you know has a record of sending people to your preferred destination. The Big Five will only tend to advertise overseas posts externally when they can't fill them with their own home-grown staff. Popular destinations are almost never advertised outside the firm.

Accountants who trained in firms without overseas links need to move to one that does have them. This could mean applying directly for a job overseas advertised by one of the UK accountancy practices, or a recruitment agency acting on its behalf. Some of the Big Five, for example, need a group of new recruits each year to go out to Bermuda to work primarily on insurance clients. They hardly ever have enough in-house candidates and always use an agency. Most of the places are allocated during a spring selection process, with appointees flying out in the late summer or autumn. A few more places may be up for grabs later in the year if the firms find they have underestimated their staffing needs.

If the direct method fails, an alternative, strategic approach is to join the UK office of an international firm with a view to impressing the partners sufficiently that they consider you for an overseas slot in a few years' time. This strategy is clearly slower to bring the desired foreign rewards and less reliable, but it may be the only option for someone who trained with a small firm. The large firms will be looking for relevant experience when filling posts overseas – participation in multinational audits, for example.

Accountants in industry or commerce can follow the same reasoning. Building up a track record within a company and consistently expressing interest in an overseas secondment may help create an opportunity that wouldn't otherwise exist. The best employers will try to give the staff the career moves and challenges they are looking for, particularly if they have already invested substantial sums in training them to a high professional level. If your immediate employer doesn't have the opportunities there, look for a company that does. Posts may be advertised directly in the usual places, such as newspapers, but signing on with a recruitment agency will maximise your chances of success.

The ultimate option is to contact employers directly, even if no jobs have been advertised. Travelling out to the chosen destination is a high-risk strategy, but will demonstrate your commitment and could turn up that longed-for job. Dedicated job hunters will write to embassies, cultivate any existing contacts, and research local companies thoroughly. The UK accounting bodies often have briefing notes for members interested in working overseas, as well as details of overseas branches and contact names. Commitment to the search, persistence and a degree of flexibility in the jobs that might be acceptable will increase the potential for success.

VSO sends volunteers overseas in three cycles – January, March, and August/September. It takes at least four months from filling in the application form to departing on a placement and VSO advises applying earlier rather than later. Couples need to allow nine to twelve months for their placement to be arranged. However, no one should apply more than a year before they are available to go abroad.

CAREER IMPACT

It is impossible to say what effect working abroad will have on an individual career. You should not overlook the potential, if temporary, damage that could be done to your CV if the quality of the work experience you gain abroad is less than that available in the UK. This can happen simply because, as a stranger in a strange land, you inevitably have some catching up to do in adapting to local surroundings. You may *want* to hit the ground running, but not be able to do so.

This isn't necessarily due to distrust of the foreigner but simply the impact of language or cultural barriers that need to be crossed before local staff perceive the newcomer as being ready for the harder assignments. In audit firms, for example, you may be given the less demanding and less exciting audit clients. Staff who return from abroad can find that the peers they left behind have handled larger and more complex deals, impressed senior bosses and carved a niche in the home office.

On the other hand, staff returning from abroad should be able to demonstrate advantages in other areas. They may have learnt a new language and may be able to use their overseas contacts as a personal selling point. The world is shrinking and whether you work in accountancy firms or companies, the ability to call on expertise in overseas locations is increasingly prized. Returning staff will also have built up contacts that could be useful in cross-border business deals. They may also be perceived as having gained in confidence and management ability, skills they strengthened by having to cope in an unfamiliar foreign environment.

Whether the plus points outweigh the minus points depends on your employer's perception and the way you sell yourself and promote your particular skills on your return. The more international in outlook the industry sector or employer, the more beneficial a period working abroad will be to your CV. In fact, some international businesses almost see it as a weakness if an individual hasn't spent time beyond the confines of the UK business community. This trend can only increase.

CASE STUDY

Keith Davis, aged thirty-one, graduated in 1987 after studying Politics at Bristol University. He took a year out to travel, returning to the UK with few immediate ideas about what career to choose. Now a qualified CIPFA member, he works at the National Audit Office.

Once back in the UK in 1988, I went to a careers fair in London and found that accountancy seemed to be the main option for someone with a non-vocational degree such as mine. That suited me in that I wanted something that was a clear profession. I wanted the security of having a recognised qualification. It gives you some harder skills you can sell and involves you in higher-level work.

I met a lot of people at the National Audit Office and felt pretty good about the organisation, that it was somewhere I wanted to work. I was attracted by its remit, that its objective is to help the nation save money and spend the taxpayer's money more wisely.

Though I joined the NAO in 1988 I became ill and deferred starting the CIPFA course until 1989, studying on block release. Now graduates qualify with the ICAEW. I didn't find the CIPFA exams easy. I failed one paper, which put me back a year, but I didn't struggle with the others and qualified in 1993.

Back in 1988, I started working on the financial audit of the Foreign and Commonwealth Office, which involved overseas visits to Embassies or High Commissions. Many of my posts here have involved travel. I worked in the FCO department for a couple of years, then moved to the financial audit of the British Council for a year or two. After that, I started value-for-money (VFM) work for the Overseas Development Administration, as it then was, looking at aid projects round the world. I have been to Japan, India three times, Thailand, Indonesia, Pakistan twice, China, Kenya twice, Morocco, Turkey, Austria, Oman, Zimbabwe and Malawi. Visits for financial audits might last a week or so, while the VFM trips tended to take up to three weeks.

I didn't ask for posts with travel, though I did request the aid-related work as I am interested in that area. I have chosen to become a VFM specialist. I prefer VFM because it lets you get into the issues that are at the heart of what organisations and agencies do. Financial accounting and auditing has to be done, but for me personally it's not the most interesting work. VFM is less procedural. You start with a blank sheet. It's more intellectual. VFM is about economy, efficiency, effectiveness. We can't question an organisation's objectives, but we can look at whether it is achieving them, whether it is organised in the best way to achieve them, all the implementational issues. We link spend to outcomes.

I am now in a central training and guidance function. I travel in this role too, as I run training courses around the world. I visited China for a week and a half last year. I train the VFM people here and provide training for overseas audit offices. I get the same satisfaction that any trainer does from getting a message across and knowing that staff can go back to their jobs with new skills they can apply.

Before starting this training role, I took a year's sabbatical and went travelling around the world. The NAO has an official career-break scheme put in place mainly for people bringing up kids. But it can also be used for staff to travel. You have to convince your line management and resource management that it is in the best interests of the office to let you go. You have to be a reasonable performer and they have to know you will come back.

To get on well here, you need certain intellectual skills. You need to be able to analyse what departments do, to understand where best to focus your work. You need political skills to understand the relationships between the NAO, the bodies we report on, and Parliament. You need to make contacts with the people you audit, interest groups, the media. Our published reports are often commented on by quality national newspapers and the specialist press.

There are always going to be some frustrations. The NAO is fairly hierarchical, but that's understandable because of the type of work it does. And there are satisfactions. When I worked in financial audit I found some major problems in some accounts which were then put right. No one else spotted them, so that was satisfying. In VFM you can put ideas forward about how to do things better. Some they take up, some they don't.

I would advise anybody to think carefully about their own reasons for going into the public sector. If they want to join the public sector because they think it's secure, a doddle, easier than the private sector, then forget it. In many areas staff are under a lot of pressure. The public sector has changed a lot over the last ten years or so. If applicants have the old preconceptions about it being undynamic and bureaucratic, they should think again.

AND FINALLY...

Accountancy isn't for everyone. It requires discipline, and it does demand some facility with numbers. The training can be tough and you may have to defend yourself from preconceptions other people still have about the excitement your chosen career provides.

 That said, an accountancy background can set you on the path to a varied, well-paid and highly portable career. If you are half-tempted to learn the art of accountancy and dabble in its magic, you might one day find yourself transformed from humble financial apprentice into a leader of British industry.

Appendix A
Qualifications

This section indicates the path to membership of the accounting, tax and other specialist bodies described in chapter 2. You should always confirm the details with the bodies themselves, since they do revise their requirements from time to time.

ASSOCIATION OF CHARTERED CERTIFIED ACCOUNTANTS

To gain the ACCA qualification, students must complete three years' approved training and pass the Association's exams within ten years from the first eligible exam sitting.

Qualifications needed to register as an ACCA student

The minimum entry requirement is two A levels and three GCSEs in five subjects, including English and Maths. Holders of the BTEC National Certificate/Diploma, NVQ Level 3 and Advanced GNVQ can also register.

Those without the necessary minimum qualifications but who are over twenty-one can apply under the Mature Student Entry Route. Mature students have four consecutive exam attempts to complete papers 1 and 3 from ACCA's Foundation Stage. Once those exams are passed, mature students are transferred to the normal student register and proceed as normal.

Exams

Foundation Stage: Accounting Framework; Legal Framework; Management Information; Organisational Framework.
Certificate Stage: Information Analysis; Audit Framework; Tax Framework; Managerial Finance.
Professional Stage: Information for Control & Decision Making; Accounting & Audit Practice; Tax Planning;

Management & Strategy; Financial Reporting Environment; Financial Strategy.

Exemptions

Any ACCA students holding a qualification higher than the minimum level required for registration, such as a relevant degree, may be entitled to exemption from some of the ACCA examinations.

CHARTERED INSTITUTE OF MANAGEMENT ACCOUNTANTS

Achieving CIMA qualification requires passing exams at four stages and completing three years' practical work experience.

Qualifications needed to register with CIMA as a student

Applicants must have at least two A levels and three GCSEs, or the equivalent, including passes in Mathematics and English Language.
Some vocational qualifications are acceptable for registration: BTEC/SCOTVEC National Certificate/Diploma in Business and Advanced General National Vocational Qualification in Business.
CIMA will also consider mature students (twenty-five years or older) with substantial practical accountancy experience but without the minimum education criteria for registration.

Exams

Each stage has four papers.
Stage 1: Financial Accounting Fundamentals; Cost Accounting and Quantitative Methods; Economic Environment: Business Environment and Information Technology.
Stage 2: Financial Accounting; Operational Cost Accounting; Management Science Applications; Business and Company Law.
Stage 3: Financial Reporting; Management Accounting Applications; Organisational Management and Development; Business Taxation.

Stage 4: Strategic Financial Management; Strategic Management Accountancy and Marketing; Information Management; Management Accounting Control Systems.

Exemptions

Exemptions are available from some of the papers in the first three exam stages for graduates with relevant degrees or some other further education, vocational or professional qualification. Careers services should have CIMA's Exemption Tracker database giving full current details.

Employers may prefer a particular method of study. Options include correspondence courses, evening classes, distance learning, sandwich or block release, day release or a combination of these. Some colleges also offer full-time CIMA courses for people without training positions. The exam syllabus is complemented by three years' practical experience which is divided into three areas: basic accounting, management accounting and financial management. To qualify for CIMA membership trainees have to keep a Record of Practical Experience which is a written account of the work experience gained and which must be verified by the employer.

CIMA operates a Training Through Partnership scheme designed to encourage more employers to provide high-quality support to trainee management accountants. Under the scheme CIMA has two levels of recognition for employer training programmes which indicate the level of support available to CIMA trainees. The basic level of recognition marks an employer as a Recognised Training Organisation providing a threshold level of support. RTOs can also apply for Professional Development Programme status if they provide training at a Best Practice level, giving trainees all the necessary practical experience required for qualification.

CHARTERED INSTITUTE OF PUBLIC FINANCE AND ACCOUNTANCY

To gain the CIPFA qualification, students must pass a series of exams and complete relevant work experience. The course is structured into four stages starting with a Foundation level, progressing through three Professional stages. At the Foundation and first two Professional stages students must submit course work and sit exams. At the Professional 3 stage candidates must undertake a practical case study exam and write a project based on a work situation.

Qualifications needed to apply for a training contract

Three GCSEs at grade A to C, plus two A levels. English and Maths must be included at either level.
The equivalent qualifications for Scotland, Northern Ireland and the Republic of Ireland and BTEC and SCOTVEC National Certificates are also accepted.
The minimum vocational qualification is a National/Scottish or General National/Scottish Vocational Qualification at Level 3 from any awarding body.

CIPFA also has two categories of entry for people without formal qualifications but with relevant work experience.
Mature Entrant. For people over twenty-one years old with three years' relevant work experience and the support of their employer.
Senior Entrant. Those over twenty-five years old with at least five years' relevant work experience can apply to start their CIPFA studies at the P1 level (skipping out the Foundation level).

Exams

Foundation: Financial Accounting; Management Accounting; Business Environment; Effective Management Skills.
Professional 1: Accounting Theory and Practice; Accounting for Decision Making; Auditing; Information Management and Control.
Professional 2: Financial Reporting; Business Strategy; Management; Treasury and Tax Management.
Professional 3: Finance and Management Case Study; Project.

Exemptions

Degrees or higher qualifications and/or relevant work experience may bring exemptions from parts of the CIPFA course.

INSTITUTE OF CHARTERED ACCOUNTANTS IN ENGLAND & WALES

To qualify as a chartered accountant requires two elements – work experience with an approved employer, and passing a series of exams.

Qualifications needed to apply for a training contract

Around 90 per cent of ICAEW trainees are graduates, but the minimum qualifications required are five GCSE/GCE passes, two of which must be A levels or equivalent (e.g. BTEC National/GNVQ Level 3). Individual employers will set their own levels – for example, some big firms will take trainees after A level, some won't.

There are four main routes to qualification:

1. A relevant degree followed by a three-year training contract and two sets of professional exams.

2. A non-relevant degree followed by a three-year training contract, a Foundation stage exam and two sets of professional exams.

3. No degree. A four-year training contract, Foundation stage and two sets of professional exams.

4. No degree. Two-year AAT at an ICAEW training office, followed by a three-year training contract. The Foundation stage may be required, plus two sets of professional exams.

Exams:– Note – the details were being reviewed in 1999.

Foundation stage: six papers: Financial Accounting and Auditing; Business Law; Economics; Introduction to Financial Decisions; Company Law; Management and Marketing.

Intermediate: five papers: Auditing and professional issues; Financial reporting; Taxation; Business planning and finance; Management information and control.
Final: four papers: Advanced auditing and financial reporting; Advanced taxation; Advanced business and financial management; Multi-disciplinary case study.

Exemptions

Trainees with relevant degrees do not have to take the Foundation stage exams. Other students may be able to gain exemption from some of the Foundation papers. For example, an economics graduate should get an exemption from the Economics paper. Approved training offices and training colleges will be able to advise on individual cases.

Most trainees find a job with an approved training office before beginning any exam training. This is the best option since most employers will pay for exam courses. But it is possible to study for the Foundation course and the Intermediate-level exams without having a training contract. Candidates for the Final-examination level must have a training contract.

INSTITUTE OF CHARTERED ACCOUNTANTS IN IRELAND

Membership requires applicants to complete a training contract, a computer-training course and pass the institute's professional exams. On registering with the institute, students receive an 'experience record' which they must complete as evidence that they have gained suitable work experience. The training contract lasts three and a half years for university graduates and three years for those who have completed a recognised postgraduate programme. All other students have to complete a four-year contract.

Qualifications needed to apply for a training contract

Though the vast majority of ICAI students are graduates, the institute has traditionally offered one- or two-year Commencement Courses for high-quality school leavers with a minimum Leaving Certificate requirement of 360 points. NCEA, NCVQ and BTEC qualifications allow the holders to study for the institute's exams without having to complete the Commencement Course.

Exams

Professional One: Introduction to Accounting; Mathematics in Business; Business Environment; Business Law.
Professional Two: Financial Accounting & Introduction to Auditing; Business Information Systems; Management Accounting and Business Finance 1; Taxation 1.
Professional Three: Advanced Financial Accounting; Auditing; Management Accounting and Business Finance II; Taxation II.
Final Admitting Examination: Auditing and the Reporting Accountant; three multi-discipline case-study based papers.

Exemptions

There are many routes to gaining exemptions from some of the exam levels. Business graduates who complete a postgraduate programme in professional accounting only have to take the Final Admitting Exam. Non-business graduates who complete similar courses become exempt from the first two institute exams. Business graduates also start the institute's exams at Professional Three, while other graduates start at Professional Two. Professional One is taken by students who have completed a one-year Commencement Course and by students with other qualifications entitling them to study for institute membership. Some Accounting Technicians and people who complete a two-year Commencement Course are exempt from Professional One.

INSTITUTE OF CHARTERED ACCOUNTANTS OF SCOTLAND

To qualify for membership of ICAS, trainees must complete a three-year training contract and pass the institute's professional exams. ICAS both teaches and examines all its students. It has training facilities in Aberdeen, Edinburgh, Glasgow and

London. Students can also train in continental Europe and attend classes at a UK centre. Employers provide paid study leave for trainees to attend the institute's block release classes which last from four to thirteen weeks. Students must maintain a logbook as proof of work experience gained during the training contract.

Qualifications needed to apply for a training contract

ICAS stands out among the accountancy bodies in that it requires all its trainees to be graduates.

Exams

Professional Examination: Multiple choice and narrative exams in auditing, financial accounting, information technology, management decision & control, business finance in the market economy, business law, and taxation.
Test of Professional Competence I: Case studies and objective testing in auditing, financial reporting, information systems, taxation.
Test of Professional Competence II: A multi-discipline case study designed to test ability to apply theoretical knowledge and practical skills to problems the newly qualified accountant is likely to encounter.

ICAS distinguishes two categories of degrees, 'fully accredited' and 'qualifying'. Fully accredited degrees grant exemption from the whole of the Professional Examination, the first-stage exam. To gain full accreditation, these degrees must contain approved courses in financial accounting, management accounting, business finance, auditing, taxation, information technology, mathematical techniques, business management, economics and business law. ICAS will supply a current list.

Any degree which does not contain the above core subjects is classified as qualifying, but there may be individual exemption from the institute's Professional Exam.

ASSOCIATION OF ACCOUNTING TECHNICIANS

To gain the AAT qualification students must complete the Association's competence-based Education and Training Scheme which consists of twenty-eight units of competence which are divided into three stages. Students have to demonstrate competence in twenty-three of the units.

The three stages are accredited by the National Council for Vocational Qualifications (NCVQ) and SCOTVEC for Scotland as National Vocational Qualifications/Scottish Vocational Qualifications (NVQs/SVQs) in Accounting. The first stage of the AAT qualification, the Foundation Stage, is accredited as NVQ/SVQ Accounting Level 2, the Intermediate Stage is Level 3, and the final Technical Stage is Level 4.

Entrance requirements for training

There are no set entrance requirements, but students are advised that they should have reasonable numeracy and literacy skills. Students with no accounting background are advised to start at the Foundation Stage.

At each stage students are assessed by a combination of Central Assessment (written and marked by the AAT) and Devolved Assessment (assessed by Approved Assessment Centres). The written papers forming the Central Assessments test the application of knowledge and understanding, not the recall of facts and figures.

Devolved Assessment by an approved assessor checks the student's competence in fulfilling graded elements of the accounting technician's role. Students compile an accounting portfolio of documentary evidence confirming their workplace activities, such as spreadsheets and reports.

To qualify for AAT membership, students must also complete at least one year's registration as a student of the Association, and complete a minimum period of one year's full-time (or equivalent) approved work experience.

Exemptions

Exemptions are granted from one or two of the stages of competence for certain relevant qualifications. For example,

the Foundation Stage will not be required for students with the following:
A level Accounting (Grade A to E)
Two other academic A levels (Grade A to E)
Advanced GNVQ Business Studies
Scottish Higher in Accountancy (Grade A to C) plus one other Scottish Higher (Grade A to C)
Three Scottish Highers in academic subjects (Grade A to C)
Irish Leaving Certificate, covering five subjects, two of which are academic subjects at honours (Grade A to D)
BTEC/SCOTVEC National or Higher National Diploma/Certificate in Business and Finance

Exemption from both the Foundation and the Intermediate Stages may be granted to students with the following:
PE1 or equivalent from one of the sponsoring bodies' qualifications (essentially the first stage of the body's professional exams)
UK degree in Accounting

INSTITUTE OF COMPANY ACCOUNTANTS

Membership of the IComA requires applicants to pass the institute's exams and complete relevant practical experience.

Qualifications needed to register as a student

The basic requirement is two A levels or the equivalent. However this may be waived for people over twenty-five years old without the minimum requirement but who have demonstrated sound ability in their careers.

Exams

The institute's entrance exams are divided into four levels with four papers in each.
Level 1: Financial Accounting 1; Quantitative Techniques; Cost Accounting; Business Law.

Level 2: Economics and the Business Environment; Business Organisation and Management; Information Technology; Taxation 1.
Level 3: Financial Accounting 2; Management Accounting; Company and Partnership Law; General Principles of Auditing and Basic Receivership and Liquidations.
Level 4: Financial Accounting 3; Financial Management *or* Professional Practice; Internal Auditing; Taxation 2.

Exemptions

Certain exemptions are available to those holding approved qualifications of a similar content and standard gained by examination. Relevant practical experience may also bring some exemptions, but there are no exemptions available from papers of Level 4.

INSTITUTE OF COST AND EXECUTIVE ACCOUNTANTS

To qualify for Associate Membership, applicants must pass three levels of exams, or earn exemption, complete at least three years' experience and prove the ability to maintain a full set of accounts, prepare management information, submit returns and effectively administer a department. Fellowship requires proof of further accounting and management ability, five years' experience and passing the fellowship-level exams.

Exams

There are three exam levels to gain Associate membership, followed by a Fellowship level, with four exam papers at each level.

Associateship:
Level 1: Accountancy & Costing; Economics; Business Law; Quantitative Methods.
Level 2: Information Technology Management; Financial Accountancy; Company Law or Local Government Law; Management.

Level 3: Cost & Management Accountancy; Advanced Accountancy; Statutory & Internal Auditing; Taxation & Tax Management.

Fellowship: Executive Accountancy & Decision-Making; Management Auditing & Control; Strategic Management; Financial Decision *or* Local Government Finance.

Exemptions

Exemptions are granted on a subject-by-subject basis to anyone with adequate experience in the application of the subject, or who holds a suitable qualification.
Holders of the BTEC Higher Certificates, graduates and other non-chartered accounting bodies may be exempt from exams at levels 1 and 2.
Chartered Secretaries may be exempt from all the Associateship examinations, except Cost and Management Accountancy.
Members of CCAB bodies may be exempt from all the Associateship exams.

INSTITUTE OF FINANCIAL ACCOUNTANTS

There are three routes to membership: by examination, by exemption or through Accredited Prior Learning. There are no set entrance requirements.

Exams

Foundation: Advanced Book-keeping.
Level II: three papers: Accounting 2; Cost Accounting; Legal Framework.
Level III: three papers: Accounting 3; Managerial Economics; Quantitative Methods in Business.
Level IV: four papers: Accounting 4; Business Taxation; Audit Techniques; Information Analysis.
Level V: four papers: Financial Management; Management Accounting; Management Strategy; Audit Regulatory Framework.

Accountancy

Exemptions

There are exemptions from the Foundation Stage for people holding the following qualifications:
One GCE A level in an academic subject plus four GCSEs at grades A, B or C, to include English Language and a quantitative subject.
BTEC National in Business *or* NVQ Level II in Accounting. Students over twenty-one years of age may also be exempt if they have the relevant accounting experience.

Other exemptions are as follows:
Level II: HNC in Business and Finance year 1
Level III: HNC in Business and Finance year 2
HND in Business and Finance year 1
Level IV: HND in Business and Finance year 2
NVQ Level IV in Accounting
ACCA Certificate Stage
CIMA Stage 3

Qualifications from other accountancy bodies may also bring exemptions.

Accredited Prior Learning

To gain membership through Accredited Prior Learning, applicants must be able to show evidence of competence. This evidence will be assessed by a Qualified Assessor. There are four main sources of evidence: prior achievement, performance in the workplace, performance in specialised set activities, and answering oral or written questions set by the assessor.

INTERNATIONAL ASSOCIATION OF BOOK-KEEPERS

The IAB allows open access to its training – there are no formal educational entry requirements.

Exams

Its manual bookkeeping examination involves three levels:
Foundation level. Aim: to test the candidate's ability to pre-

pare and record cash, credit, payroll and stock movement in the books of account.

Intermediate level. Aim: to test the candidate's ability to prepare and account for cash and credit transactions, to record capital transactions and to prepare financial accounts, reports and returns.

Final level. Aim: to test the candidate's ability to draft financial statements, to prepare statutory documentation and returns, to undertake cost analysis and control, to set up specialised accounts and to understand the requirements for the capital structure of companies and the admission of new partners and the treatment of goodwill.

Exemptions

Exemptions are available for people holding the following qualifications:
Foundation level: RSA Stage I or LCCI Elementary or equivalent in Bookkeeping or Accounts.
Intermediate level: GCSE or RSA Stage II or LCCI Intermediate or equivalent in Bookkeeping or Accounts.
Final level: RSA Stage III (Advanced), or LCCI Higher, or the Intermediate stage of other recognised senior professional examining bodies, or A level or equivalent at Grades A, B, or C in Bookkeeping or Accounting.
Candidates aged nineteen or over with at least three years' approved business experience can also gain exemption from the Foundation level.

CHARTERED INSTITUTE OF TAXATION

Associate membership requires passing the Associate exams, and completing three years' professional experience. Many of those who choose to study for the CIoT's exams have already gained another qualification, generally in accountancy or in law. But the minimum entry requirements are as follows:
Two subjects (not craft) at A level GCE exams with grades A to D; *or*
Passes in five subjects at Higher Level Scottish Certificate of

Education exams, at grades A to D, though grades A or B must be achieved in at least three subjects; *or*
Passes in five subjects at Honours or Higher Level in the Republic of Ireland Leaving Certificate at grades A to C with grades A or B in at least three of those subjects; *or*
One A level GCE exam at grade A to C and two subjects at Advanced Supplementary level at grades A to D; *or*
Four subjects at Advanced Supplementary level at grades A to D.
Candidates who have passed the examination of the Association of Taxation Technicians are also eligible for entry to the CIoT exams.

Exams

Candidates for both the standard and the VAT specialist routes are required to have a knowledge of the basic principles of law and there will be a legal element contained in the tax exam papers.

The standard exam route includes four papers:
I Tax Administration, Professional Responsibilities and Ethics
II Personal Tax and Trust Taxation
III Business Taxation
IV Practical Implications, Interaction and Tax Planning

The VAT specialist routes includes three papers:
I Tax Administration, Professional Responsibilities and Ethics
II VAT Principles and Planning
III VAT Case Studies

ASSOCIATION OF TAXATION TECHNICIANS

To apply for admission to membership, candidates must have completed a minimum of eighteen months' current practical experience working in tax, and have passed the ATT's examinations.

Qualifications

Requirements for registering as a student

Individuals must have passed:
either at least four subjects at GCSE or GCE Ordinary level at Grade A, B or C;
or at least three subjects at GCE Advanced Supplementary level at Grade A to C
or at least two subjects at GCE A level at Grade A to E
or GNVQ Level 3 at pass with merit and above.
Passes must include English Language and an acceptable numerate subject.
Membership of the Association of Accounting Technicians can be used as an alternative to the exam requirements above.

Exams

The exams cover tax and law and accounting, with two papers in each. The papers are Personal Taxation; Business Taxation; Principles of Law; Principles of Accounting.

ASSOCIATION OF CORPORATE TREASURERS

The minimum entry requirements to study for Associate Membership are five GCSEs or five GCEs, which should include English and Maths and be at grade C or higher. Students are also expected to have a working knowledge of double-entry bookkeeping. The Membership qualification builds on the Associate syllabus.

Exams

The Associate syllabus is tested in six exam papers: I Accounting Practice & Introductory Economics; II Financial Analysis; III Corporate Taxation; IV Business Law; V Money Management; VI Corporate Finance and Funding.
The Membership syllabus is tested in three exam papers: VII Corporate Financial Management; VIII Advanced Funding and Risk Management; IX Treasury Management.

Exemptions

Exemptions are available for candidates who have completed the examination of the following bodies:
Paper I: the Chartered Institute of Bankers
Papers I–IV: ACCA; CIMA; CIPFA; ICAEW; ICAS; the Institute of Chartered Secretaries and Administrators

INSOLVENCY PRACTITIONERS ASSOCIATION

The IPA offers the Certificate of Proficiency in Insolvency, a qualification for those who work in the insolvency field, but who do not wish to sit the Joint Insolvency Examinations Board (JIEB) exam, or who wish to use it as a stepping stone to the JIEB exam. Minimum entry requirements are five O levels or GCSEs or equivalent in any subjects and two years' full-time insolvency experience, or five years' full-time insolvency experience.

Exams

CPI exam
The exam comprises one three-hour paper of three parts, requiring knowledge of corporate and personal insolvency with an emphasis on liquidations and receiverships.

Joint Insolvency Examinations Board
In order to become a licensed Insolvency Practitioner you have to pass the JIEB exam. Members of recognised professional bodies with one year's experience or those who have passed the Entry Level Examinations of the IPA are eligible to attempt the JIEB exams.

Recognised professional bodies include the ICAEW, ICAS, ICAI, ACCA, The Law Society and The Law Society of Scotland.

The JIEB exam consists of three papers:
Paper 1: Liquidations
Paper 2: Receivership, Administrations and CVAs
Paper 3: Personal Insolvency

Appendix B
Accountancy Degrees

An accountancy degree is by no means essential for a career as an accountant. In the UK none of the professional training bodies requires students to have studied a relevant degree. The best advice is probably to choose the subject that really interests you. Also bear in mind that skills such as language or IT ability are valued in the business world, and there are many combined degrees that include such subjects.

The following universities offer degrees in accountancy. Further information about related courses, such as in Finance, and combination options is given in the *Universities and Colleges Admissions Service Handbook*. Details of course content should be checked before making any application.

The University of Aberdeen, Aberdeen AB24 3FX; tel. 0122 427 3504

University of Abertay Dundee, Bell Street, Dundee DD1 1HG; tel. 01382 308080

The University of Wales, Aberystwyth, Ceredigion SY23 2AX; tel. 01970 622021

Anglia Polytechnic University, Victoria Road South, Chelmsford CM1 1LL; tel. 01245 493131

University of Wales, Bangor, Gwynedd LL57 2DG; tel. 01248 351151

The University of Birmingham, Edgbaston, Birmingham B15 2TT; tel. 0121 414 3344; Internet www.bham.ac.uk

Blackburn College, Feilden Street, Blackburn BB2 1LH; tel. 01254 551440

Bolton Institute of Higher Education, Deane Road, Bolton BL3 5AB; tel. 01204 528851/900600

Bournemouth University, Talbot Campus, Fern Barrow, Poole, Dorset BH12 5BB; tel. 01202 524111

Bradford and Ilkley Community College, Great Horton Road, Bradford, West Yorkshire BD7 1AY; tel. 01274 753026

University of Brighton, Mithras House, Lewes Road, Brighton BN2 4AT; tel. 01273 600900

University of Bristol, Bristol BS8 1TH; tel. 0117 928 9000; Internet www.bris.ac.uk

University of the West of England, Bristol, Frenchay Campus, Coldharbour Lane, Bristol BS16 1QY; tel. 0117 965 6261

Brunel University, West London, Uxbridge, Middlesex UB8 3PH; tel. 01895 274000

The University of Buckingham, Hunter Street, Buckingham MK18 1EG; tel. 01280 814080

University of Wales, Cardiff, PO Box 494, Cardiff CF1 3YL; tel. 01222 874404

University of Central England in Birmingham, Perry Barr, Birmingham B42 2SU; tel. 0121 331 5000

University of Central Lancashire, Preston PR1 2HE; tel. 01772 201201

City University, Northampton Square, London EC1V 0HB; tel. 0171 477 8000

Coventry University, Priory Street, Coventry CV1 5FB; tel. 01203 631313

Croydon College, Fairfield, Croydon CR9 1DX; tel. 0181 686 5700

De Montfort University, Leicester, The Gateway, Leicester LE1 9BH; tel. 0116 255 1551

Accountancy Degrees

University of Derby, Kedleston Road, Derby DE22 1GB; tel. 01332 622222, prospectus requests ext. 1980

University of Dundee, Dundee DD1 4HN; tel. 01382 344028

The University of Durham, Old Shire Hall, Durham DH1 3HP; tel. 0191 374 2000

The University of East Anglia, Norwich NR4 7TJ; tel. 01603 456161; Internet www.uea.ac.uk/

University of East London, Barking Campus, Longbridge Road, Dagenham, Essex RM8 2AS; tel. 0181 590 7722

The University of Edinburgh, Edinburgh EH8 9YL; tel. 0131 650 1000; Internet www.ed.ac.uk/

The University of Essex, Wivenhoe Park, Colchester CO4 3SQ; tel. 01206 873666

University of Exeter, Exeter, Devon EX4 4QJ; tel. 01392 263030

Farnborough College of Technology, Boundary Road, Farnborough, Hampshire GU14 6SB; tel. 01252 391212

University of Glamorgan, Treforest, Pontypridd, Mid Glamorgan CF37 1DL; tel. 01443 480480

University of Glasgow, Glasgow G12 8QQ; tel. 0141 330 4575; Internet www.gla.ac.uk/admissions/

Glasgow Caledonian University, City Campus, Cowcaddens Road, Glasgow G4 0BA: tel. 0141 331 3000

University of Greenwich, Wellington Street, Woolwich, London SE18 6PF; tel. 0181 331 8590

Heriot-Watt University, Edinburgh, Riccarton, Edinburgh EH14 4AS; tel. 0131 449 5111; Internet www.hw.ac.uk/

University of Hertfordshire, College Lane, Hatfield, Herts AL10 9AB; tel. 01707 284000

The University of Huddersfield, Queensgate, Huddersfield HD1 3DH; tel. 01484 422288

Accountancy

The University of Hull, North Humberside HU6 7RX; tel. 01482 466100

The University of Kent at Canterbury, Canterbury, Kent CT2 7NZ; tel. 01227 827272

Kingston University, River House, 53–7 High Street, Kingston upon Thames KT1 1LQ; tel. 0181 547 2000

Lancaster University, Lancaster LA1 4YW; tel. 01524 65201; Internet www.lancs.ac.uk/

University of Leeds, Leeds LS2 9JT; tel. 0113 233 3999

Leeds Metropolitan University, Calverley Street, Leeds LS1 3HE; tel. 0113 283 2600; Internet www.lmu.ac.uk

University of Lincolnshire and Humberside, Humberside University Campus, Central Admissions Unit, Milner Hall, Cottingham Road, Hull HU6 7RT; tel. 01482 440550

The University of Liverpool, PO Box 147, Liverpool L69 3BX; tel. 0151 794 2000

Liverpool John Moores University, Roscoe Court, 4 Rodney Street, Liverpool L1 2TZ; tel. 0151 231 5090/5091; Internet www.livjm.ac.uk

London Guildhall University, The Course Enquiries Unit, 133 Whitechapel High Street, London E1 7QA; tel. 0171 320 1616

London School of Economics and Political Science, University of London, PO Box 13401, Houghton Street, London WC2A 2AE; tel. 0171 405 7686

Loughborough University, Loughborough, Leicestershire LE11 3TU; tel. 01509 263171

University of Luton, Park Square, Luton, Beds LU1 3JU; tel. 01582 734111

The University of Manchester, Manchester M13 9PL; tel. 0161 275 2077

The Manchester Metropolitan University, All Saints, Manchester M15 6BH; tel. 0161 247 2000

Middlesex University, White Hart Lane, London N17 8HR; tel. 0181 362 5000

Napier University, 219 Colinton Road, Edinburgh EH14 1DJ; tel. 0131 444 2266

Nene College of Higher Education, Park Campus, Boughton Green Road, Northampton NN2 7AL; tel. 01604 735500

University of Newcastle upon Tyne, Newcastle upon Tyne NE1 7RU; tel. 0191 222 6138

University of Wales College, Newport, PO Box 101, Newport, South Wales NP6 1YH; tel. 01633 432432

The North-east Wales Institute of Higher Education, Plas Coch, Mold Road, Wrexham LL11 2AW; tel. 01978 290666

University of North London, Holloway Road, London N7 8DB; tel. 0171 753 3272

University of Northumbria at Newcastle, Ellison Building, Ellison Place, Newcastle upon Tyne NE1 8ST; tel. 0191 227 4777

Norwich City College, Ipswich Road, Norwich, Norfolk NR2 2LJ; tel. 01603 773140

The University of Nottingham, University Park, Nottingham NG7 2RD; tel. 0115 951 5151

The Nottingham Trent University, Burton Street, Nottingham NG1 4BU; tel. 0115 941 8418

Oxford Brookes University, Gipsy Lane, Headington, Oxford OX3 0BP; tel. 01865 483040

University of Paisley, High Street, Paisley, Renfrewshire, Scotland PA1 2BE; tel. 0141 848 3000

University of Plymouth, Drake Circus, Plymouth PL4 8AA; tel. 01752 600600

University of Portsmouth, University House, Winston Churchill Avenue, Portsmouth PO1 2UP; tel. 01705 876543; Internet www.port.ac.uk

Accountancy

The Queen's University of Belfast, University Road, Belfast, BT7 1NN; tel. 01232 273079; Internet www.qub.ac.uk

The University of Reading, PO Box 217, Reading RG6 2AH; tel. 01734 875123; Internet www.reading.ac.uk/UG

The Robert Gordon University, Schoolhill, Aberdeen, Scotland AB10 1FR; tel. 01224 262000

The University of Salford, Salford M5 4WT; tel. 0161 745 5000

The University of Sheffield, Sheffield S10 2TN; tel. 0114 222 2000; Internet www.shef.ac.uk/uni/admin/admit/

Sheffield Hallam University, City Campus, Pond Street, Sheffield S1 1WB; tel. 0114 225 5555

The University of Southampton, Southampton SO17 1BJ; tel. 01703 595000

Southampton Institute, East Park Terrace, Southampton SO14 0YN; tel. 01703 319000

South Bank University, 103 Borough Road, London SE1 0AA; tel. 0171 815 8158; Internet www.sbu.ac.uk

Staffordshire University, College Road, Stoke on Trent ST4 2DE; tel. 01782 294000

The University of Stirling, Stirling FK9 4LA; tel. 01786 473171

The University of Strathclyde, Glasgow G1 1XQ; tel. 0141 553 4170

University College Suffolk, Suffolk College, Ipswich, Suffolk IP4 1LT; tel. 01473 255885

University of Sunderland, Unit 4C, Technology Park, Chester Road, Sunderland SR2 7PS; tel. 0191 515 3000; Internet www.sunderland.ac.uk

Swansea Institute of Higher Education, Townhill Campus, Townhill Road, Swansea SA2 0UT; tel. 01792 481263

University of Teesside, Middlesbrough, Cleveland TS1 3BA; tel. 01642 218121

Thames Valley University, St Mary's Road, Ealing, London W5 5RF; tel. 0181 579 5000; Internet www.tvu.uk/

University of Ulster, Coleraine, Co. Londonderry, Northern Ireland BT52 1SA; tel. 01265 44141

The University of Warwick, Coventry CV4 7AL; tel. 01203 523723

University of Wolverhampton, Wolverhampton WV1 1SB; tel. 01902 321000; Internet www.wlv.ac.uk

ACCOUNTING HNDs

University of Abertay Dundee, Bell Street, Dundee DD1 1HG; tel. 01382 308080

Bell College of Technology, Almada Street, Hamilton, Lanarkshire, Scotland ML3 0JB; tel. 01698 283100

Croydon College, Fairfield, Croydon CR9 1DX; tel. 0181 686 5700

University of Glamorgan, Treforest, Pontypridd, Mid Glamorgan CF37 1DL; tel. 01443 480480

University of Wales College, Newport, PO Box 101, Newport, South Wales NP6 1YH; tel. 01633 432432

University of North London, Holloway Road, London N7 8DB; tel. 0171 753 3272

University of Northumbria at Newcastle, Ellison Building, Ellison Place, Newcastle upon Tyne NE1 8ST; tel. 0191 227 4777

The Scottish College of Textiles, Netherdale, Galashiels TD1 3HF; tel. 01896 755511; Internet www.scot.ac.uk

TRAINING FOR PROFESSIONAL EXAMS

There are a huge number of training colleges and private training companies across the country running courses directly targeted at getting students through the exams set by various accountancy bodies. Some employers may recommend a particular college or training company, or automatically send their staff there. If you are left to choose for yourself, your best bet is to contact the relevant professional body for a list of recommended colleges.

Appendix C
Useful Addresses

CHAPTER 2
ACCOUNTANCY BODIES AND RELATED INSTITUTIONS

Association of Accounting Technicians, 154 Clerkenwell Road, London EC1R 5AD; tel. 0171 837 8600; fax 0171 837 6970; e-mail aatuk@dial.pipex.com
Publishes a guide to its Education and Training Scheme and a list of Approved Assessment Centres.

Association of Chartered Certified Accountants, 29 Lincoln's Inn Fields, London WC2A 3EE; tel. 0171 396 5800; e-mail student.recruitment@acca.co.uk; Internet www.acca.co.uk
Produces brochure on the ACCA qualification and career prospects, plus a full list of colleges offering ACCA courses.

Association of Taxation Technicians, 12 Upper Belgrave Street, London SW1X 8BB; tel. 0171 235 2544
Produces a brochure explaining how to become a member, a leaflet detailing the benefits of membership and a list of colleges providing tuition in the ATT's exam.

Chartered Institute of Management Accountants, 63 Portland Place, London W1N 4AB; tel. 0171 637 2311; fax 0171 631 5309; e-mail mw-registry@cima.org.uk for registering as a student; Internet www.cima.org.uk. Produces guides on the management accountant career, college lists and information on registering as a CIMA student.

Chartered Institute of Public Finance and Accountancy, 3 Robert Street, London WC2N 6BH; tel. 0171 543 5600; fax

0171 543 5700; Internet www.cipfa.org.uk. Produces a student guide, information on the senior entrant's scheme, CIPFA's syllabus and regulations, and a training vacancy listing.

Institute of Chartered Accountants in England & Wales, Chartered Accountants' Hall, PO Box 433, Moorgate Place, London EC2P 2BJ; tel. 0171 920 8100; fax 0171 920 0547; Internet www.icaew.co.uk. Produces several guides covering training as a chartered accountant, organisations offering training contracts, academic qualifications and examinations, training outside public practice, names of local accountancy careers advisers.

Institute of Chartered Accountants in Ireland, Chartered Accountants' House, 87/89 Pembroke Road, Dublin 4; tel. 00 353 1 6680400; fax 00 353 1 6680842; e-mail charternet@icai.ie; *or* 11 Donegall Square South, Belfast BT1 5JE; tel. 01232 321600; fax 01232 230071; e-mail icai@ dnet.co.uk; Internet www.icai.ie. Produces a brochure explaining the career opportunities for an Irish CA and details of the procedure to win qualification, as well as a list of training vacancies in approved firms.

Institute of Chartered Accountants of Scotland, 27 Queen Street, Edinburgh EH2 1LA; tel. 0131 225 5673; fax 0131 247 4872; Internet www.icas.org.uk. Produces several guides for potential trainees explaining the life of a chartered accountant, the institute's prospectus and its exam syllabus.

Institute of Company Accountants, 40 Tyndalls Park Road, Bristol BS8 1PL; tel. 0117 973 8261; fax 0117 923 8292. Produces a leaflet explaining the history and role of the institute, details of its examination syllabus, distance learning courses and its own journal, *Company Accountant*.

Institute of Cost and Executive Accountants, Tower House, 141–149 Fonthill Road, London N4 3HF; tel. 0171 272 3925; fax 0171 281 5723. Produces general information on the qualification.

Institute of Financial Accountants, Burford House, 44 London Road, Sevenoaks, Kent TN13 1AS; tel. 01732 458080; fax 01732 455848. Produces brochure introducing its qualification and the steps to membership.

International Association of Book-keepers, Burford House, 44 London Road, Sevenoaks, Kent TN13 1AS; tel. 01732 458080; fax 01732 455848. Produces leaflet detailing benefits of membership and qualification requirements.

SPECIALIST BODIES

The Association of Corporate Treasurers, 12 Devereux Court, London WC2R 3JJ; tel. 0171 936 2354; fax 0171 936 4685. Publishes a brochure explaining its qualification and details of the exam syllabus.

Chartered Institute of Taxation, 12 Upper Belgrave Street, London SW1X 8BB; tel. 0171 235 9381; fax 0171 235 2562. Produces a brochure explaining how to become a member, and a list of colleges providing suitable tuition courses.

Insolvency Practitioners Association, Moor House, 119 London Wall, London EC2Y 5ET; tel. 0171 374 4200; fax 0171 588 7216. Produces information on the institute and its Certificate of Proficiency in Insolvency, as well as information about the JIEB exams.

BIG FIVE AUDIT FIRMS

Each firm produces a recruitment brochure which gives a flavour of the organisation's culture and career opportunities.

Arthur Andersen, 1 Surrey Street, London WC2R 2PS; tel. 0171 438 3000; Internet www.arthurandersen.co.uk

Deloitte & Touche, Hill House, 1 Little New Street, London EC4A 3TR; tel. 0171 936 3000; Internet www.deloitte-touche.co.uk

Ernst & Young, Becket House, 1 Lambeth Palace Road, London SE1 7EU; tel. 0171 928 2000; Internet ernsty.co.uk

Accountancy

KPMG, 8 Salisbury Square, London EC4Y 8BB; tel. 0171 311 1000; Internet www.kpmg.co.uk

PricewaterhouseCoopers, 1 Embankment Place, London WC2N 6NN; tel. 0171 583 5000; Internet www.pwcglobal.com

GOVERNMENT ORGANISATIONS AND AGENCIES

District Audit, Nicholson House, Lime Kiln Close, Stoke Gifford, Bristol BS12 6SU; tel. 0117 923 6757; fax 0117 979 4100. Produces information pack on a career in District Audit.

National Audit Office, Information Centre, 157–197 Buckingham Palace Road, London SW1W 9SP; tel. 0171 798 7264. Provides information on NAO careers.

CHAPTER 3

Women In Accountancy can be contacted through any of the six CCAB accountancy bodies: Association of Chartered Certified Accountants, Chartered Institute of Management Accountants, Chartered Institute of Public Finance and Accountancy, Institute of Chartered Accountants in England & Wales, Institute of Chartered Accountants in Ireland, Institiute of Chartered Accountants of Scotland.

CHAPTER 5

Voluntary Service Overseas, 317 Putney Bridge Road, London SW15 2PN; tel. 0181 780 2266/1331; Internet www.oneworld.org/vso/. Produces booklet to inform potential volunteers about the selection process and nature of the overseas work and experience.

Appendix D
Further Reading

PROFESSIONAL JOURNALS AND MAGAZINES

Magazines published by the accountancy bodies for their members provide an insight into the latest hot topics facing the profession. Most contain a mix of news items and longer features including interviews with senior accountants – all useful stuff to see what an accounting career would involve, and to provide ammunition for job interviews.

Accountancy, monthly journal published by the Institute of Chartered Accountants in England & Wales, 40 Bernard Street, London WC1N 1LD; tel. 0171 833 3291; fax 0171 833 2085; e-mail: postmaster@theabg.demon.co.uk; Internet www.accountancymag.co.uk

Accounting Technician, monthly journal of the Association of Accounting Technicians. Published by Reed Business Publishing, Quadrant House, The Quadrant, Sutton, Surrey SM2 5AS; tel. 0181 652 4800; fax 0181 652 4748.

CA Magazine, monthly magazine for the Institute of Chartered Accountants of Scotland, 27 Queen Street, Edinburgh EH2 1LA; tel. 0131 225 5673; fax 0131 247 4830; e-mail ca.magazine@icas.org.uk

Company Accountant, bi-monthly journal published by the Institute of Company Accountants and sent to all its members and students. Editorial and advertising offices, 40 Tyndalls Park Road, Bristol BS8 1PL; tel. 0117 973 8261.

Management Accounting, published by the Chartered Institute of Management Accountants, 63 Portland Place, London W1N 4AB; tel. 0171 917 9256; fax 0171 436 1282; e-mail cimalis@cima.org.uk. Eleven issues a year. CIMA also publishes a special supplement for management accounting trainees, called *CIMA Student*.

TRADE MAGAZINES

Accountancy Age, weekly newspaper aimed at all qualified accountants. Published by VNU Business Publications, VNU House, 32–34 Broadwick Street, London W1A 2HG; tel. 0171 316 9000; fax 0171 316 9250; e-mail accountancy_age@vnu.co.uk; Internet accountancyage.vnu.co.uk

OTHER

Added-value professionals – Chartered Accountants in 2005. Report published by the Institute of Chartered Accountants in England & Wales (see Appendix C for address) looking at the future career prospects for its members. The report gives a useful insight into the challenges facing chartered accountants.

Also available in the Guardian Careers Guide Series from Fourth Estate:

JOBFINDER

Christine Ingham

The essential guide to finding employment for those entering the job market and those planning a career change.

The world of work has changed: most people will work for several employers in the course of their careers. To the new, would-be employee, or someone wanting to shift career, this is an uncertain universe in which to pitch one's qualifications. It demands new skills, a willingness to be adaptable and an initial resourcefulness in learning where opportunities are to be found and how best to exploit them. This guide will provide essential answers to all the most difficult questions that may arise in this new climate.

£8.99   ISBN: 1 85702 630 6

INTERVIEWS

Christine Ingham

How to prepare yourself fully for the most important part of the job application process: the face-to-face interview.

The interview is of prime importance. It's the moment when you must impress personality, fluency, interest and some guile if necessary. This book tells you how to prepare for every eventuality. It breaks down the kind of questions you are likely to meet and gives examples of the most typical. It discusses the different strategies you might adopt when faced with a panel of interviewers rather than a single one. Also, crucially, it explains how you should use the interview for your own ends: how to take control of the direction it is following, and how to put the interviewer on the spot.

£8.99   ISBN: 1 85702 627 6

NEWS JOURNALISM

Nick Varley

The guide to working with the news: from local paper reporter to satellite television newscaster.

Media studies courses have blossomed and competition for places on them – never mind jobs afterwards – is intense. This book is targeted at those people for whom the news is their specific ambition. The interchangeability of skills and the flexibility now required of news journalists so that they can flit between radio and television are essential qualities to have. The book examines the core abilities required of a good news reporter and news editor, and the pitfalls of a profession that is built around the contact book.

£8.99   ISBN: 1 85702 693 4

LAW

Fiona Boyle

The guide to all legal careers from the most modest legal-aid barrister to the most affluent corporate solicitor.

The law continues to attract waves of applicants in search of a career in one of the classic professions. This guide outlines all the various specialisations available within the law. It looks at which areas of work are expanding and which contracting, follows the careers of successful young lawyers, looks at paralegal openings and examines the flexibility of a legal qualification and its suitability for other areas of work. Focusing primarily on careers in the law in England and Wales, it also includes details of the different legal set-ups in Scotland and Northern Ireland and advice on European and overseas career opportunities.

£8.99   ISBN: 1 85702 631 4

SECONDARY EDUCATION

Kathy Vandyck

The guide to careers in all secondary education establishments, including advice on training.

A spate of early retirements, combined with the Labour government's pledge to reduce class sizes, means that recruitment in secondary education will be intensive over the next couple of years. This guide examines likely openings in every subject area, while highlighting the growing need for management and analytical abilites among teachers faced by the financial pressures and competition of league tables.

£8.99   ISBN: 1 85702 750 7

FURTHER AND ADULT EDUCATION

Peter Mayhew-Smith

A vital sector, newly emphasised by government as essential for stimulating and sharpening a professional workforce, this guide is to careers in teaching in adult and further education.

Outside full-time education there seems to be nothing but a confusion of acronyms. This book explains, quantifies and appraises the entire further education sector including: FE colleges, Colleges of Tertiary Education; 6th Form Colleges; Adult Education Colleges; Community Education Services; TECs; Supply Agencies; Private Training Agencies; and the newly designated University of Industry. With advice and guidance on pay, career structure, the various employers in the sector, training, getting started, choosing what to teach and at what level, pastoral work, counselling and the full range of the teacher's duties, and shifting within and out from the sector this book presents a complete and comprehensive overview of careers in adult and further education.

£8.99   ISBN: 1 85702 545 8

All Fourth Estate books are available at your local bookshop or newsagent, or can be ordered direct from the publisher.

Indicate the number of copies required and quote the author and title.

Send cheque/eurocheque/postal order (Sterling only), made payable to Book Service By Post, to:

> Fourth Estate Books,
> Book Service By Post,
> PO Box 29, Douglas
> I-O-M, IM99 1BQ

Or phone: 01624 675137

Or fax: 01624 670923

Or e-mail: bookshop@enterprise.net

Alternatively pay by Access, Visa or Mastercard

Card number ☐☐☐☐☐☐☐☐☐☐☐☐☐

Expiry date ....

Signature ....

Post and packing is free in the UK. Overseas customers please allow £1.00 per book for post and packing.

Name ....
Address ....
....
....

Please allow 28 days for delivery. Please tick the box if you do not wish to receive any additional information. ❏

Prices and availability subject to change without notice.